Patron Behavior in Libraries

A Handbook of Positive Approaches to Negative Situations

Beth McNeil and Denise J. Johnson

American Library Association
Chicago and London
1996

Cover design by Tessing Design

Text design and composition by Publishing Services, Inc.
in ITC Galliard on a Xyvision/L330

Printed on 50-pound Glatfelter, a pH-neutral stock,
and bound in 10-point cover stock by Edward Brothers, Inc.

The paper used in this publication meets the minimum requirements of American National Standard for Information Sciences—Permanence of Paper for Printed Library Materials, ANSI Z39.48-1992. ∞

Library of Congress Cataloging-in-Publication Data

Patron behavior in libraries : a handbook of positive approaches to
negative situations / [edited by] Beth McNeil and Denise J. Johnson.
p. cm.
Includes bibliographical references and index.
ISBN 0-8389-0662-1
1. Libraries and readers—United States. 2. Libraries—United
States—Security measures. I. McNeil, Beth. II. Johnson, Denise J.
Z711.P338 1996
025.5—dc20 95-40639

Printed in the United States of America.

00 99 98 5 4 3 2

Contents

Introduction v

Part I

Which Patrons Pose the Most Challenges and Why?

1 Down and Out in the Reading Room: The Homeless in the Public Library 3
Bruce A. Shuman

2 Mentally Ill Patrons 18
Charles A. Salter and Jeffrey L. Salter

3 Opposites Attract: Young Adults and Libraries 44
Patrick Jones

4 Older Adults: Problems and Needs 55
Linda Marie Golian and Linda Lou Wiler

5 Deinstitutionalized and Disabled Patrons: Opportunities and Solutions 65
Fay Zipkowitz

6 Problems with Patrons in the Academic Library 75
Emerita M. Cuesta

Part II

What Are the Issues?

7 Crime in Academic Libraries 87
Mary M. Harrison, Alison Armstrong, and David Hollenbeck

8 Legal Issues regarding Library Patrons 95
Katherine Malmquist

9 Sexual Harassment in the Library 106
Denise J. Johnson

10 Sexual Behavior in Libraries 122
Denise J. Johnson

Part III

What Are the Solutions?

11 Active Listening: Alleviating Patron Problems through Communication 127
Nathan M. Smith

12 Developing and Implementing a Patron Behavior Policy 135
Linda A. Morrissett

13 Literature on Library Patrons: An Annotated Guide 150
Beth McNeil

Contributors 154

Index 157

Introduction

The literature of patron problems in libraries extends back to some of our earliest modern professional literature. Articles have been written detailing specific problems, workshops on problem patrons are a staple of library conferences, and a few books have been published on the subject. The handful of books devoted to patron problems are useful and illuminating, yet no one book has been published which deals with the subject from a broad perspective, with a view to describing the various problems presented by a diverse patron population and prescribing solutions to disruptive patron behavior.

In compiling this book, we gathered a diverse and talented group of librarians to write about the subject with which they are most familiar. We want to offer useful information to public librarians, academic librarians, children's librarians, and special librarians. It is our aim to assist librarians who need help in staff training, in dealing with various types of patron behavior problems, in establishing procedures for handling problems and complaints, and in researching patron problems in libraries.

The book's contributors include library science faculty, university librarians, special librarians, and public librarians. Each section includes a collection of chapters pertaining to the theme of the section. In part I, for instance, there is a chapter on understanding and coping with homeless patrons in the public library written by Bruce Shuman, the author of the 1984 title, *River Bend Revisited: The Problem Patron in the Library.*

The problem of homelessness is briefly discussed in several other chapters, due to the pervasive effects of this societal problem on libraries. Because libraries are public buildings and free of charge, they have always attracted a large number of people with no other place to go. Because homeless people often lack adequate bathing facilities and because the ranks of the homeless are swollen with deinstitutionalized and mentally ill individuals, there are many problems associated with their use of libraries. Library staff members must cope with the humanitarian and informational needs of the homeless, without neglecting the needs of their more traditional users. It is a delicate balancing act: serving the needs of library users who are there more for warmth and comfort than for information and serving the needs of information seekers who are sometimes frightened or put off by the presence of the homeless. Shuman's chapter helps to clarify the issues of serving the homeless in the public library and provides library staff members with guidelines for developing policies and procedures to deal with the problems.

Also in the first section is a contribution from Jeffrey and Charles Salter, "Mentally Ill Patrons." Mentally ill patrons pose many of the same problems for library workers as the homeless. After encountering mentally ill patrons, who sometimes behave strangely or may even seem threatening, some patrons are reluctant to visit the library or to allow their adolescent children to spend time in the library unattended. Mentally ill patrons may also cause difficulty for staff members, through inappropriate behavior or conversation. The Salters' chapter will help library staff sort out the innocuous from the potentially dangerous situations and respond appropriately. Jeffrey Salter is a library administrator at the Shreveport Public Library. His brother Charles is a practicing psychologist. They are the authors of *On the Frontlines,* the 1988 book on dealing with problem patron behavior.

Young adults, while not in and of themselves problems, often are perceived as difficult patrons by people who find them noisy, disruptive, or disrespectful. Patrick Jones, the manager of the Tecumseh branch of the Allen County Public Library (Fort Wayne, Ind.), has written extensively on young adult topics and is in demand as a workshop speaker on the subject of library service to young adults. His chapter, "Opposites Attract: Young Adults and Libraries," describes typical behavior encountered in dealing with young adults and offers useful insight into the developmental causes of behavior that might seem problematic to the uninitiated. Jones provides practical advice on developing more skillful interactions and a greater understanding of young adults.

At the other end of the patron age spectrum is a chapter on library services to older adults, contributed by Linda Marie Golian, serials department head for Florida Atlantic University Libraries in Boca Raton, and Linda Lou Wiler, the library development officer at Florida Atlantic University. Both Golian and Wiler have developed library programming for older adults. While older adult patrons are not typically considered problematic, there are special needs and problems in providing library service to older patrons. Problems of vision, mobility, and hearing are among the health-related problems significantly affecting older people and, consequently, their needs for library services and materials. This chapter offers a variety of constructive tips and techniques, as well as a thoughtful discussion of the issues.

Often when library workers discuss or write about problems with patrons the focus is on dealing with the problems, not on serving the patrons who have problems. A number of the chapters approach patron problems from a service rather than a disciplinary stance. A good example of this approach is found in Fay Zipkowitz's chapter on serving the disabled and deinstitutionalized. Zipkowitz, associate professor of library science at the University of Rhode Island, provides useful ideas and inspires library workers to view adherence to the Americans with Disabilities Act as an opportunity, not a burden.

The last chapter in part I, contributed by Emerita Cuesta, deals with problem patrons in academic libraries. Academic libraries are not sheltered by the ivory towers surrounding them from the problems encountered in public libraries. Those who work in academic libraries will attest to this fact. Cuesta, who is currently in charge of access services at Hofstra University, writes from her experiences in three academic libraries.

Issues are the subject of part II; one, crime, is an increasing problem in libraries. Some of the headlines that appeared in *American Libraries* during the last year include: "Sex Books Vandalized in Oregon" (*AL* 5/95, p.393), "Students Charged in Library Vandalism" (*AL* 1/95, p.16), "Hostages Safe after Siege at Salt Lake City PL" (*AL* 4/94, p.294), "Death Sentence for Librarian's Killer" (*AL* 12/94, p.980). Some libraries are developing plans to beat crime, and the chapter "Crime in Academic Libraries" can help all libraries do the same. The coauthors of this chapter are Mary M. Harrison, Alison Armstrong, and David Hollenbeck. At the time of writing, Harrison was the head reference librarian at the University of Nevada, Las Vegas, where Armstrong is instruction librarian and Hollenbeck is director of public safety/chief of police. Harrison is now head of the education and social sciences library at Southern Illinois University, Carbondale.

There are legal issues involved in dealing with patron behavior in libraries. Library policies must take into account patron rights while protecting the library's ability to provide information and services. Katherine Malmquist, associate director of the law library at Cleveland-Marshall College of Law, has written a chapter on the legal rights and responsibilities of patrons and libraries, and provides tips for writing policies that will hold up in court, should they be legally challenged.

For most people, sexual harassment is an issue that involves supervisors, staff, and coworkers, but in public service professions sexual harassment is more likely to come from the customers and patrons. What are the responsibilities of the employer in these situations? How can staff members be trained to respond effectively to harassing behavior? And what is considered sexual harassment? For a clarification of sexual harassment issues in libraries, see the chapter authored by Denise Johnson, access services librarian at the Bradley University Library.

Also contributed by Johnson is a chapter on sexual misconduct in libraries. The chapter describes the ways that public buildings are used for inappropriate sexual behavior and how staff can detect and prevent such behavior in their buildings.

In conceptualizing this book, we envisioned a book that librarians and staff members could use to help solve problems sometimes posed by patrons. We asked contributors to focus on practical approaches to the problems described. The chapters in the first two sections of the book indeed address that challenge. Chapters in part III deal exclusively with problem-solving methods. Nathan M. Smith, life sciences museum librarian at Brigham Young University, has contributed a chapter on improving and enhancing communication skills to effectively control problems and reduce confrontational communications with patrons. Linda Morrissett, circulation supervisor at Western Kentucky University Libraries, takes a proactive stance in dealing with problems in her chapter on behavior policies. The section concludes with a review of the recent literature on problem patrons, authored by Beth McNeil, reference services librarian at Bradley University.

It is our hope that you will find this book a useful guide, regardless of your role or job in the library. We have tried to address the issues affecting workers at every level: library administrators, managers, librarians, and paraprofessional staff.

The problems faced in dealing with patron behavior in libraries affect all of us, but most pertinently, those who serve the public directly. We all need each other's support and ideas to effectively combat problems and make our workplaces the kind of places we would like to visit as patrons.

Denise J. Johnson and Beth McNeil

I

Which Patrons Pose the Most Challenges and Why?

1

Down and Out in the Reading Room: The Homeless in the Public Library

Bruce A. Shuman

Ah, look at all the lonely people; where do they all come from?
—The Beatles (from "Eleanor Rigby")

The Homeless

The homeless have always been part of the American landscape, especially in urban areas, and the problem seems to grow incrementally every year. More and more of them seek refuge in public libraries.

It would be rash and overly simplistic to seek or target a single reason or cause for the perceived upsurge in the number of urban homeless, or for the apparent severity of their plight. A number of well-documented explanations, however, do come to mind:

Federal Inaction

Twelve years of the Reagan and Bush administrations did little to build or renovate affordable housing for the homeless, even though it is estimated that more than 15,000 homeless live in Washington, D.C., some dwelling close enough to walk to the Capitol or the White House. Congress is not blameless, however, since there was only lukewarm support for housing legislation in both houses during this period. Under the Clinton administration, expectations were raised, perhaps unrealistically. As with many things, there is a sharp difference between lip service and good intentions on one hand, and legislation and commitment of funds on the other.

Deinstitutionalization

Both as a cost-cutting measure and a new trend in psychotherapy, outpatient drug therapy supposedly renders institutionalization unnecessary, and consequently, mental institutions have greatly reduced their inmate populations. This trend has cast onto the streets many seriously ill and unprepared people, some dangerously psychotic, who now must fend for themselves. Public mental institutions were, of course, no respite from society's rigors. Although the quality of care for the indigent mentally ill in such hospitals and treatment centers varied from barely adequate to appalling, at least patients had food, shelter, and usually, access to medication. Out on the street, however, it is a mean world, and difficult, if not impossible, for someone to find help. Many homeless people cannot or do not ask for help, or finally quit asking. Others weaken and die of hunger, cold, disease, crime, or natural causes. A few have violent psychotic incidents injuring or killing either themselves or other people.

Out on the streets, the formerly institutionalized and certifiably psychotic mix indistinguishably with the normal, hard-luck down-and-outers, and there is no way to tell the harmless from the potentially dangerous. Society lumps them together—untouchables, all—and most of the rest of us find ourselves wishing that they would go away.

Unemployment/Low Minimum Wage

There is a growing number of so-called working poor, who are scarcely better off than the homeless or the chronically unemployed. They are trying to do the right thing—work, contribute, pay taxes—but since they are employed, they are ineligible for welfare or Medicare. Most of us cannot imagine supporting ourselves on $4 and change per hour, *before* taxes, let alone trying to support other family members. The simple fact is for many Americans it cannot be done. Paying the rent, putting food on the table, and paying taxes can use the entire paycheck, such that a small emergency (such as an unexpected trip to the hospital emergency room in an ambulance) may lead to a deficit situation, throwing formerly housed people out on the streets.

This trend has created a new class in our ostensibly classless society: the "new poor," who, as victims of sweeping social service cutbacks, are unable to get jobs and have no hope of affordable housing. They are driven out onto the streets where they live hand to mouth and as best they can. Included in this group are the "formerly employed," who are no longer eligible for unemployment benefits and are bereft of hope for future rehabilitation. Predominant in this group are racial minorities and a growing segment of the female and young population.

Intolerable Living Conditions and Crime

The government, often out of necessity or expediency, houses welfare recipients in substandard available housing, at times packing several families into a meager one-family space riddled with vermin and sometimes vandalized by other neighborhood residents. Some people then become homeless by preference, finding their assigned living quarters intolerable, and the streets less hazardous than the projects and urban homeless shelters where people are frequently assaulted and robbed of their few remaining possessions.

Jurisdictional Fights

As silly as it may seem, some people are rendered homeless because well-intentioned functionaries of federal, state, county, and municipal jurisdictions who are trying to provide adequate housing, cannot agree on who has responsibility for the homeless. Homeless people are often homeless because they fell through the "cracks" in the network that is supposed to provide for their basic necessities.

Indifference

Indifference may be the saddest reason of all, yet may also be the most prevalent. There is an increasingly rueful note of truth to the old gag, "there's a lot of apathy around here, but then, who cares?" We walk past the homeless on the streets, avoiding eye contact, appalled by their scruffy appearance and powerful odors, and dehumanize them in our minds. Maybe we allow ourselves the virtuous emotion of pity for a brief moment, or perhaps even thrust a coin or two into an outstretched filthy hand, and then we hurry on about our business, wishing that our urban landscape were not cluttered with these unsightly pieces of human jetsam. Or maybe we mutter "get a job!" when they shuffle up to us seeking charity, as though homeless persons without the wherewithal to groom themselves could just drag a comb across their heads, neaten their attire, march into an employment agency and be sent out instantly to a job. On Sunday, we might hear our clergy solemnly intone how we are all our brothers' keepers, but we have problems of our own, after all. Besides, the idea of equality among all people has always struck us as an abstraction. The way the world really works is often a clear-cut case of "I've got mine, and it's terribly sad about you." But we fail to call it selfishness. We believe that it is simply the result of hard work and circumstance that we have clean, well-lighted homes and refrigerators full of food. We know there are others who do not, but thinking about them too long or too hard makes us uncomfortable. It is easier to think of pleasant things.

The homeless are in every urban location and throughout the country. There are millions of them, and the reasons for their conditions are numerous. Unfortunately, many of them are children under ten years of age. They wander the city streets, trying to get fed and stay warm in the winters. Maybe that is why there are many homeless in places like Los Angeles and Miami, since in the north during winter, the homeless are cold and hungry. In more temperate climates, they are only hungry. Sitting on a warm steam grate during a Northern winter affords a bit of comfort, but there is a sort of social Darwinism at work here. Only the fittest get the primo spots. To challenge someone stronger or armed with a weapon for a warm place to rest risks a beating, or worse.

But when the homeless weary of the streets and seek the shelter of buildings, where can they warm up and snooze a bit in a relatively clean, well-lighted place? It is easier to list the places they *cannot* go. In every city, downtown commercial buildings have security personnel whose responsibilities include shooing away the undesirables.

Most other warm places cost money to enter. Unless you can pay the price of a movie, you cannot seek shelter in a theater. Even then, theater managers take a dim view of vagrants and sleepers in their movie houses. Restaurants do not appreciate those who sit in one place for hours, nursing a doughnut and a cup of coffee. They especially do not like it if a lack of personal hygiene causes other customers to avoid a seating area, or exit hastily, or enter, change their minds, and leave quickly without ordering. So where can the homeless go?

The public library is often the only place.

The Homeless and the Public Library

There is nothing new about the homeless in the library. If it seems that more has been written in the past two decades on the topic than ever before, that is an accurate perception. It is also fair to point out that homelessness has grown in proportion to recent urban economic problems, and so it is not unusual that more homeless people are hanging out in the library than ever before, or at least since the end of the Great Depression of the 1930s. So, if someone is homeless, cold, and looking for a few hours of respite from physical and mental problems, the library seems an ideal haven.

Before we segue into a discussion of the problems of libraries concerning the homeless, there is one important member-group of the "cast" of this drama who has not been heard from: the homeless. Let's listen to one representative voice directly affected by library policies regarding the homeless. (We call him "Larry," because there are more homeless males than females but it could as easily have been "Loretta"). Let Larry describe in his own words why he frequents the library every day.

> Larry: Had a home once, but no more. And a job, a paycheck, and people who loved me, or leastways looked glad to see me now and then, but no more. What happened to me came on slowly at first, helped along by a couple bad habits an' addictions, and then quicker. One day (now don't be askin' me which one—my mind's a mess) I found myself out on the street: no job, no home, cold and hungry, just the clothes on my back, an' an ol' rusty shoppin' cart I found someplace in an alley, to keep my other stuff in. Bathrooms is a problem, 'cause the restaurants and stores 'round here don't like to see me come in and head that way. An' the only way to sleep in a bed (well, really a cot) is to check in at the shelter (if I can get in, that is) and take my chances that some crazy druggie ain't gonna put a knife in me while I'm sleepin' or make off with my shoes.
>
> Gave up a long time ago on ever again havin' a place to call my own. Now I'm ahead of the game if I can get somethin' to eat and don't nobody hurt me. Spend my days shufflin' around, rootin' in garbage cans and dumpsters for food; you'd be amazed if I tole ya what folks throw away, and just as amazed at what I've ate. I could tell ya, but I don't wanna make you sick. Winter nights are pure hell: sittin' cross-legged over a steam grate, or walkin' all night to keep warm, so's I don't turn into a popsicle. I got a few things here in this cart, but they's all stuff that other folks threw away, an' I was lucky enough to find 'em. Not much: blanket, tarpaulin, extra shirt, two more pairs o' underpants, an' some old shoes I found in the dumpster out behind the YMCA. Trouble with havin' a cart is that I have ta hide it from all the other poor sad bastards out here tryin' to survive. Some nights, when it's just too cold to stay out, I flop in that hot, smelly, overcrowded shelter, when I can find a place. See, the first sixty or so people in line get the cots. Ever'body else gets turned away, 'cause ain't room for all of us. So ever' day, at 5:30 sharp, I gotta be outside that door, ready to bull my way through it before the

guy inside counts to a hunnerd an' ten, or it's the streets for me that night.

Out on the streets, you lose track of time (if you lucky, that is), an' you drink (when drink's available, hopin' it ain't gonna kill you or make you blind). Sometimes, I drink to keep warm, or to keep my spirits up, but mostly I drink to forget all the stuff that's on my mind, and to get to sleep in some doorway or alley. Used to bother me, sleepin' in doorways, but not no more. Now, I guess I'm so far gone that I hardly notice the looks people givin' me. It's only when a cop or somebody puts a boot into me that I notice. Sometimes, street punks throw blue-tip matches at guys lyin' aroun' in doorways, trying to light 'em up. Even heard about a guy sleepin' it off what got doused with gasoline and set afire. Helluva way to wake up. "Burned beyond recognition" is what the paper called it. Trust me: them kind of words is not what I want to read about some other guy in the mornin' paper—an' I sure don't want nobody else to read 'em about me.

Well, now that I'm up and stirrin', guess I'll plan my day. Too cold for the park, so I need another plan. Lessee, here. What to do . . . what to do. . . .

A Challenge to Libraries

American public libraries are beset with many problems, many of them relating to, or symptomatic of, inadequate or shrinking budgets. One problem, however, that seems to be societal rather than specific to public libraries is that of the homeless. Homeless persons with nowhere else to go naturally gravitate to public buildings as a haven from the streets, a place with public restrooms, and quiet rooms where one can read, socialize, and on occasion, sleep without the requirement of paying for the privilege. There are related problems to homelessness stemming from lack of access to proper sanitation and hygiene, lack of interest in same, and sometimes mental illness.

All of these worries affect the library directly, as well as all who spend time in it. If homelessness is a great social and personal tragedy, the consequences and ramifications for persons trying to run a public library are immense. The homeless sometimes fall into the general and amorphous library classification of "problem patrons," along with thieves, exhibitionists, and persons whose behaviors are annoying and worrisome, yet completely legal. It is, however, important to remember that not all homeless persons *are* problem patrons, and that not all problem patrons are homeless. And even if you consider the homeless to be, always and everywhere, problem patrons, it is still possible to divide them into either two groups (harmless vs. innocuous) or three (harmless, innocuous, and "who the heck knows?").

Those in charge of security have attempted to classify problem patrons into groups or broad headings and deal with them as classes. For instance (see figure 1), a division based on the perceived threat to others in the immediate vicinity:

Class I	**Class II**	**Class III**
Dangerous (very serious)	**Who Knows? (serious but...)**	**Nuisances (annoying but harmless)**
armed	drunk	begging
sexually deviant	narcotized	malodorous
emotionally disturbed	homeless	eating
predatory	soliciting	time monopolizing
combative	defacing	laundering
felonious	rulebreaking	loud talking, laughing
delinquent	belonging to gang	defacing
committing arson	highly emotional	latchkey
vandalizing	staring	whispering, humming
threatening	exhibitionist	lonely
touching	zealous, preaching	sleeping
child molesting	"acting weird"	hyperactive
lawbreaking	politically incorrect	voyeuristic
paranoid	physically ill	amorous (consensual)
drug-intoxicated	hallucinating	coughing
openly hostile	bringing pets	eating
verbally abusive	continual pacing	knuckle-cracking
drug selling	loitering	chattering

Figure 1. Classes of Problem Patrons in Public Libraries with Representative Behaviors

Defining some of the conditions listed in the figure, many of which pertain to the homeless, will obviously depend on circumstances, or even on one's subjective distinction among such poorly defined terms as "eccentric," "highly emotional," "emotionally disturbed," and "psychotic." In the absence of on-site psychiatric evaluation of individuals, most such classifications become nothing more than impromptu judgment calls by untrained observers and will vary accordingly with the individual observer. Still, there are forms of triage that security and staff can apply with a degree of consistency. A person classified as "physically ill" may require only a routine call to 911, or on the other hand, may be a strong risk to himself or herself or others present. The library staff member, however, does not always have the time and opportunity to analyze facts and render a measured judgment. Sometimes, an instant decision is both necessary and desirable.

Despite lurid headlines in the library journals and the general news media, most of America's homeless frequenting libraries are persons down on their luck, seeking only warmth or daytime respite from the elements, predators, police, or boredom. They are generally harmless, even though considered "nuisances" by library staff and other patrons. It is true that many of the homeless cannot avoid, or are uninterested in controlling, extreme body odor, a severe problem for others in the library building. Library literature is full of news items and lawsuit proceedings on the conflicting rights of persons to have free access to library materials versus other persons seeking the same access in non-toxic air. Yet libraries have not been able to develop a policy that is unambiguous in its definition of "smelling bad," and most policies on prohibited behaviors make no mention of odor.

The following is a typical listing of the prohibitions of a big-city public library, an example of an attempt to ban specific behavior problems.

Your cooperation is requested in refraining from:

1. Loitering or sleeping on library property
2. Gambling, soliciting, or campaigning on library property
3. Eating and drinking in the library
4. Use of typewriters and playing of radios, tape players, and televisions without use of personal earphones in authorized areas
5. Fighting, running, or "horseplay"
6. Use of loud, obscene, or abusive language
7. Smoking except in authorized areas
8. Bringing in animals other than guide dogs
9. Inappropriate dress, for example, bare chests and feet
10. Carrying of weapons or dangerous objects
11. Public drunkenness or use of alcohol
12. All sexual acts and sexually deviant behavior
13. Mutilation or damage of library materials, equipment, and property
14. Use of drugs, hallucinogens, and other chemical substances
15. Placing feet on library furniture
16. Leaving children unattended.

Notice what's missing? The list, as sweeping as it may seem in its coverage, says nothing about patron odor at all. A judge in the notorious *Kreimer* case said he was unable to support the efforts of a library to throw a malodorous patron out and keep him out, because the library had not clearly defined the offense so that it could be determined whether or not the homeless man had crossed the line of unacceptable behavior. The behavior of the man which made him highly unpopular with staff and patrons alike was irrelevant to the "odor" issue. As the judge said, "if you define 'speeding' as driving too fast, there is plenty of room for interpretation." So, apparently, it is with smelling bad.

Several libraries have tried to deal with the problem of odor in more quantifiable terms other than calling it "bad." Library security guards have attempted to grapple with such vague language by developing rules, for example, that if a guard can smell a patron's body odor at a distance of six feet, that patron may be evicted from the library. Any lesser distance and the offense is not severe enough to merit the patron's removal from the building. Such a definition, however, is arbitrary and extremely vague, due to many variables, such as the guard's sense of smell, difficulty in estimating "six feet," the direction of air currents in the room, and the nature of the odor. Moreover, it is highly doubtful whether such a criterion of acceptability, if challenged, would stand in a court of law.

> Larry: I'm always dirty and most times hungry. On automatic pilot, that's what I call it. Point of ever' day is to get through it, alive and fed. Nights, try to find a warm, safe place to sleep, tucked away from the bushwackers that's always out there. Don't hurt nobody, and look out for y'self and you'll get by, somehow. Winter's the test. If you can survive the winter, you can do the rest. But, like I said, what's the damn point? Keep losin' track of what day it is—hell, it don't matter much, anyway. Life's a routine—look for food, go to the library, stay away from people, don't talk if you don't have to, lie down on whatever's handy that's softer than the pavement, try to keep warm, and be ready to defend yourself against folks even more whacked out or desperate than y'self.

Homelessness is a national problem, and while not strictly an urban problem, it is predominantly so. It is not a problem specific to the victims, those personally and directly affected by having no place to sleep or live. It is, for libraries, everybody's problem. More importantly, homeless people cannot be classed as some monolithic entity. They do not all act, react, or think the same way. Some are, admittedly, seriously and dangerously ill, and that illness may be physical, mental, or even emotional. Others are quite "normal" in the sense of being average in intelligence or perception. What they frequently share is a syndrome of conditions from which they cannot easily escape, for it is the human condition. The homeless get hungry, they experience too much of cold or heat, dampness and dryness, they experience fear of others and anxiety for their safety. They feel suspicion and sometimes anger toward police and social workers, or the variety of people who approach them offering help, seeking to rehabilitate their bodies, their work skills, or, sometimes, their souls. A sense of hopelessness is pervasive among the homeless and it takes more than charity or policy to make that feeling go away.

Through bitter, first-hand experience, the homeless person is disinclined to trust "do-gooders" beyond accepting charity when it is offered, and not even then, in some cases. Many are proud and disdain charity, subsisting only on what they can provide for themselves, while others have a talent for panhandling and telling hard-luck stories to affluent passers-by, making a surprising (and tax-free) wage through preying on the guilt or discomfort of others. Feeding themselves adequately is often a day-long occupation, and alcohol, when available, is both a comfort and an enemy.

Some homeless disdain traditional services designed for their benefit. Some years ago, a very controversial ordinance in New York City required that, on nights when the outside temperature fell below 32° Fahrenheit, police officers were obliged to collect homeless persons and convey them to public shelters, whether they chose to go there or not. There were, at the time, numerous incidents of fistfights, biting, gougings, and reported police brutality. Even though it was manifestly decreed for the good of the homeless, there was still the matter of their rights as citizens, a matter still unresolved.

Library Policies and the Homeless

The homeless make use of the public library as a place to take shelter from the streets. Depending on the prevailing weather, they warm up, cool off, sleep when they can, use restroom facilities, and bathe when no one prevents them from doing so. Some actually read or use library materials, while others use these materials as props to justify their presence in the library.

Most homeless people feel a sense of entitlement to use the library as citizens and former or occasional taxpayers, and see no reason why they should be treated differently from other library visitors. With a few exceptions, they are meek and inoffensive, knowing that their continued ability to enter and use the building corresponds to their comportment and behavior. Many, if they could choose to become so, would be transparent or invisible, able to enter and move about the library without attracting the notice of staff, guards, or other patrons. Those few who come in angry, defiant, flouting the rules, or threatening others, are the ones who grab all the headlines, but most others desire to be left alone in anonymous silence.

The library, of course, lacks the luxury of just ignoring many of the homeless because of their demonstrable lack of personal hygiene. Long and costly legal battles have been fought over whether personal aroma should disqualify someone from admission and full use of the library. The following are some of the arguments made for requiring malodorous or otherwise obnoxious persons to leave, and another list in favor of toleration. The arguments in favor of barriers to the homeless are:

1. The library exists for the purpose of satisfying the information and reading needs of its patrons, in a pleasant, comfortable atmosphere. Anyone not in the library for "library purposes" is fair game for expulsion orders. Any visitor to the library who seriously interferes with the normal functioning of the facility, either by nuisance or threat, is a problem for all and may be dealt with in the same way as any other nuisances or threats.
2. Unwashed persons, because of their appearance or aroma, can make use of library materials difficult for others. One malodorous patron can prevent other library patrons from entering a room. Why should one smelly customer be permitted to foul the air of dozens or hundreds of others who keep themselves reasonably clean?
3. Mental or emotional illness is often part of the homeless person's history or condition. Public safety concerns may permit libraries to evict persons who may misbehave as a prudent precaution, even if they are not misbehaving at the moment. To adopt an attitude of "we don't holler until we're hurt" is potentially reckless and irresponsible on the part of library administration.
4. Library staff cannot leave a building, as can patrons, to escape from offensive-smelling or offensive-acting people. Dealing with the homeless daily tends to arouse negative feelings in employees, leading to high turnover or a decline in morale. A demoralized staff is an inefficient one. Moreover, listening to complaints about the homeless, yet being unable to do anything about them, is stressful on staff.

The arguments against barriers to the homeless are:

1. The homeless have rights like anyone else, and it is unfair and discriminatory to treat them differently because they are unfortunate or lacking the comforts of others.

2. As it may be illegal to treat homeless persons differently, the library could be in jeopardy from lawsuits demanding both compensatory and punitive damages if homeless persons are denied admittance (or ejected from) the library.
3. Libraries tend to be centrally located, warm and inviting places, and thus attract the homeless. Community agencies that deal with the homeless are often severely overtaxed, short-staffed, and hamstrung by laws, rules, and citizen complaints. Urban police may complain that they have higher priorities in their workdays than rousting nuisance patrons from public libraries. Besides, police are disinclined to place smelly vagrants in their police cruisers for transport to shelters or jail. The library, even where it is forbidden to ban or regulate the behavior of "problem patrons," can perform an important community service by identifying and reporting apparently homeless persons to proper authorities, thus preventing needless suffering and even death.
4. Recent trends in mental health treatment have prescribed library visits for those persons classified as "harmless" among the formerly institutionalized. The library provides them the opportunity to associate with "normal" persons as a form of therapy. The public library thus serves as a link in the chain of rehabilitation and reintegration of such persons into the mainstream of society.

Larry: Sunday's a bad day—library's closed. Gotta find some other place to be. Like they say, ain't no such thing as a free lunch. Shelter may give me a cot for the night, but gotta get out by 8 o'clock. Mission may give me food, but there's a price—gotta listen to one of Ol' Holy Joe's sermons, while pretendin' to pray. Ain't but one place I really enjoy goin', and that's the public library. But down to the library, they just told me yestiddy mornin' that I'm banned—no longer welcome to enter, they said! Say I don't smell nice. Well, duhhh! Lessee them fancy-pants librarians wear the same clothes for weeks an' come up smellin' like rose petals. Ain't right! Little 'nuff pleasure in my life as it is, and now they done sent me away from the onliest place I actually enjoy being in. Is that fair, or what? Do them library fools think I'd look (an' smell) this way if I had a choice? But I got no choice. Hard to wash up when you livin' in a refrigerator box under the expressway.

Yeah, the library's the place, all right. I mean, I'm a taxpayer—sort of—or I usta be, anyway—and I got rights. The library's a daytime shelter when they kick me out of the nighttime one, and a lot safer than hanging out in the park, or in those dirty, dark alleys where I spend my time in the nice weather. I love that library, even if it don't love me back. First off, it's warm inside. That's the important thing. And muggers and street gangs usually stay clear, so I can relax my guard a bit. But once I make it past the door, the trick is to take down a book or magazine and put it in front of me, like I'm reading, whether that's what I'm doing or not. Then I got a couple choices while I sit there: actually read, or just turn the pages and look at the pictures, or try to sneak a nap, as long as I'm careful about snoring, and as long as the walkin' guard on duty isn't one of them mean ones that shakes you fit to break your neck, sayin' something about how sleepin' in the library is strictly forbidden, and tellin' you to get the hell out.

But the library ain't open but 56 hours a week, nowadays. Budget cuts, they say. That works out to 9 to 9 a couple of days a week, 9 to 6 four other days, and four hours on Sunday afternoon. Used to be more, but times are tough for ever'body, I guess. Anyway, I figured it out one time: there's 168 hours in a week, and I can spend about one-third of 'em inside where it's warm and dry. I mean, sittin' inside, lookin' at the rain and snow through a plate-glass window sure beats hell outta humpin' from dumpster to dumpster, scavengin' alleys for useful stuff. Aside from them security dudes, though, the onliest thing bad about the library is that I have to hide my shoppin' cart full of stuff before I go in. They get real funny about me wheelin' in there with my cart.

Next winter, if I live, maybe I'll go to Florida. They got palm trees there, an' flowers all year roun', an you can sleep on the beach. There, I wouldn't freeze, anyway, like I'm gonna do tonight. Well, I better get on down to the back of the Safeway, 'cause it's about the time they throw away all the bread from yesterday, and I wanna get a loaf or two before the others get there. Hope my cart with the blankets is still where I hid it down behind the recycling plant. Jeez, it's gonna be cold out there! Look at that wind! Might be Monday again before I'm warm. Paper said somethin' 'bout snow.

Too bad about Larry, you may be saying after reading this, a genuine shame, but what's it got to do with me? I've got a job and a home. The frightening fact is that millions of Americans (the ones we call the "working poor," for example, struggling along on minimum wage jobs and without any form of health care) are only a few paychecks away from sharing Larry's fate. And if you are victimized by homelessness, you could well be seeking the shelter and warmth of a public library next year, or the one after that.

Some Vexing Questions for Librarians

Many difficult and vexing questions are raised concerning the rights and privileges of homeless persons in the library. These questions may be legal, ethical, merely practical, or all three. For example:

If library policy stipulates that those wishing to take out library materials must have home addresses to be eligible for borrowing privileges, what is the proper response to a homeless (and thus address-less) person requesting a library card?

When does tolerable eccentricity become abnormal behavior which justifies, or even necessitates, some kind of action? Where do you draw the line? Are there any lines, or should there be? What criteria should be used, and who makes the judgment call?

When does enforcement of reasonable rules become harassment of individuals?

Is it appropriate to designate a room for the homeless and require that they use only that room while in the library building?

Do library staff have the right or responsibility to address homeless persons regarding their perceived lack of compliance with the rules of acceptable conduct or appearance?

Does denying equal access to information in the library to any subset of the community equal discrimination and denial of group members' civil rights?

How literally should we interpret the meaning of the word "public" in the name of the public library? Does the word "public" mean that anyone is entitled to be in the building?

Should "informational need" be the criterion of admission to the library? Who is qualified to determine the nature and scope of an "informational need," and whether specific behaviors qualify as such?

Is there a difference between access to information and access to the library itself? How (and by whom) is this determined, and how does this impact the homeless?

What about persons who don't smell noticeably bad, but who are obviously loitering or hanging around the library all day?

Are psychological barriers regarding access to libraries for the homeless an important issue, along with physical and legal ones?

Can a library that deals harshly and decisively with its homeless honestly say that it is "reaching out" to its public?

This list of questions is far from exhaustive and merely illustrates some of the nettlesome issues of dealing with the homeless and the public library. Inevitably, there are far more questions raised than answered. It is still valuable and useful, however, to consider the questions, even if answers tend toward "whatever you can live with, given your unique circumstances." In any event, more research on the homeless is both necessary and desirable to render better, more equitable, and just decisions.

2

Mentally Ill Patrons

Charles A. Salter and Jeffrey L. Salter

Reasons for Fear of the Mentally Disturbed

Among the types of patrons who generate problems within the library, mentally ill patrons typically cause the greatest concern for the library staff. While criminals may cause more fear, they are usually considered intruders rather than patrons. Mentally ill persons actually may be patrons but can generate a high level of staff apprehension and uncertainty regarding appropriate response. There are many reasons for this anxiety among staff.

Lack of Understanding

Most library staff have virtually no idea what causes mental illness, and the unknown always tends to produce anxiety. Such staff wish the person would just leave or "straighten himself (or herself) out" and cease all "odd" behavior. On the other hand, staff who know something about the causes of mental illness are more likely to demonstrate compassionate and sensible approaches to coping with such behavior problems.

Problem Behavior

Certain forms of mentally disturbed behavior can appear frightening. For example, patrons with ***hallucinations*** (sensations and perceptions which are not real) may converse angrily with imaginary persons or creatures. Patrons with ***delusions*** (beliefs which are not true) may accuse library staff of being foreign spies, devils, or even creatures from other planets. *Sociopaths,* those with a weak or nonexistent moral code, may boldly lie about other patrons or staff; they may even try to exploit them financially, socially, or sexually. Such behaviors as these rightly cause concern among library staff as well as other patrons. Understanding the different types of mental illness, however, can help keep such concerns in perspective.

Unpredictability

The "normal" person tends to keep responding to his or her environment much as he or she has in the recent past. But some mentally ill persons may abruptly shift behavioral styles without warning or without any obvious trigger from the environment. Manic-depressives, for instance, may appear manic at times, bubbling over with energy, enthusiasm, and unbounded confidence. But then suddenly they may appear depressed, sad, and withdrawn, with a sense of hopelessness and worthlessness. In either case, the precipitating events for these mood swings are unclear. Once library staff realize that patron "X" is wildly unpredictable they may dread dealing with him or her. On the other hand, when staff learn to recognize the *patterns* of the symptoms that go together, they can better comprehend unusual behavioral changes.

Uncertain Risk

All of the above factors generate anxiety and produce risks which are difficult to evaluate. Depending on the type of mental illness, there may be a risk of violence directed at other patrons or staff, there may be irrational outbursts of emotional or disturbing content, or there may be ceaseless repetition of bizarre behavior, such as face-rubbing, writing of weird notes, and so forth, with no direct threat to others. Not knowing what to expect or when to expect it can naturally keep workers and regular patrons on edge. But staff who develop a greater understanding of mental illnesses and related behaviors can better evaluate the potential risk of an odd behavior becoming a dangerous behavior.

Uncertainty about Responding

A naive employee with little or no knowledge about the mentally ill may feel very anxious when trying to respond to such situations as those described. He or she may feel paralyzed with doubt, fearful of making things worse in an attempt to make them better. The lack of a firm but compassionate response, however, will often only exacerbate the problem. With training, staff can be better prepared to cope with difficult behavior when it occurs, possibly containing it before it becomes more serious.

Allaying Staff Fears of the Mentally Ill

Library managers have a responsibility to ensure that their staff members are prepared to deal with the kinds of situations posed by mentally disturbed individuals. Proper training can diminish each of the sources of anxiety. Training helps staff to understand the causes of mental illness, what types of disturbed behavior to expect, how to assess possible risks posed by mentally ill patrons, and how to defuse precarious situations.

In-Service Training

All public libraries should have some form of in-service training for staff, particularly for less experienced staff who deal directly with the public. At a minimum, managers should keep a supply of self-study materials including this book. Ideally, occasional seminars will be offered during work time to discuss potential problems and solutions. Such sessions should be interesting and practical, with discussion of events that have actually occurred and perhaps role-playing ways they *were* handled and *should* have been. If the budget permits, outside speakers can conduct more extensive workshops.

Courses in Psychology

Managers should at least provide some employees with formal instruction in psychology, such as regular undergraduate or graduate courses that deal with psychopathology, theories of personality, and behavior modification. Ideally all staff will have the option to pursue continuing education, but if the budget doesn't permit such latitude, a few should participate on a selective basis. If even one staff member develops an introductory knowledge of mental illness, he or she can serve as a resource person for the rest of the staff. This person can develop and maintain the in-service training program and materials for the others.

Staff Support

Employees who have had a difficult encounter with a mentally ill patron will often need support afterwards. At a minimum, supervisors should allow the front-line staff to blow off steam, discuss what happened, and express their feelings about it. Encourage them to write up the incident for the record while their memories are still fresh (detailed later in this chapter). This is probably not a good time, however, for formal instruction on how to deal with such problems in the future. Each involved person should be allowed to discuss the problem freely, listened to carefully without criticism, and provided some emotional support. In serious cases where the worker has suffered actual violence or a perceived threat of violence (or for any other reason appears severely upset over the experience), the opportunity for professional counselling should be offered.

Knowledge Required for Adequate Coping

In whatever training programs offered, it is important to include subjects such as those that follow. But realize that the discussion that follows is necessarily oversimplified to provide only the briefest of introductory overviews. Entire series of books have been written on psychopathology and no explanation as short as this can do the subject complete justice. On the other hand, library workers clearly do not need a professional education on this topic. A brief introduction will suffice as long as employees realize its limitations and that they are not experts after reading it.

Reasons for the Increase in Disturbed Patrons in Libraries

Many an impatient librarian or library staff member has wondered aloud, "Why are so many 'psychos' invading our facilities? Why are they all picking on us?" The answer is complex. Before the 1970s, people who were clearly mentally disturbed were routinely locked up in state mental hospitals. Whether they claimed to be normal or not, whether they wanted to be treated or left alone, they could be admitted if a family member and psychiatrist deemed it advisable. If no family member was available to make such a recommendation, the police could arrange for hospital admission based on the decision of a judge and a psychiatrist.

Beginning in the mid-1970s, however, legal precedents shifted the focus to patients' rights, i.e., patients could not be hospitalized against their will unless they were clearly a danger to themselves or to others. At the same time, state budget cuts, advances in therapy, and a drive for community mental health care (among other factors) led to a strong move to deinstitutionalize mental patients. Within a few years, the United States went from locking up the mentally disturbed, whether they wanted it or not, to the opposite extreme of thrusting them on the local community even if the patient did not want to be released and had nowhere to go.

Unfortunately, the planned network of community mental health centers to provide services to the newly released mentally ill never materialized on a large scale. Therefore, the net result of these massive societal changes was to leave many unsupervised and mostly untreated mentally ill persons on their own on the streets. It was estimated in 1988 that 92 percent of the two million seriously mentally ill Americans *were not* institutionalized.[1] Many of these people and many more who are only moderately mentally ill often gravitate to public areas where they are less likely to be expelled or "hassled" by authorities. A large proportion end up in libraries.

Causes of Mental Illness

A librarian who has no idea where mental illness "comes from" may tend to blame the disturbed patron or even treat him harshly. Therefore, it is important that all staff who deal directly with patrons have at least an embryonic idea of what causes mental illness. There are two primary types of causes of mental illness—*organic* and *functional.*

Organic Illnesses

Organic illnesses are those caused by biological factors, usually with objectively measurable damage to the nervous system. For instance, genetic factors can lead to malformation or progressive deterioration of the nervous system. The former ensures that full development of the healthy brain will never take place, while the latter over time brings a worsening loss of memory and self-control. Persistent or intense alcohol drinking, drug abuse, or excessive exposure to environmental contaminants can chemically induce permanent brain damage. Various brain infections, diseases such as arteriosclerosis, or accidental injury to the brain (for example, bullet penetrations or concussions from accidents) can cause permanent damage to the brain. Often such destruction will limit only perceptual or muscular capacity, but sometimes it is associated with personality disturbances and odd behavior.

Functional Illnesses

Functional illnesses are those caused by psychological or social factors, with no apparent physical damage yet resulting in abnormal changes in behavior. Prolonged, unrelieved stress, for example, can lead to counterproductive attempts at coping which lead to bizarre behaviors. For instance, people deprived of a warm, loving environment throughout childhood, especially if also subjected to abuse, may develop problems with personality adjustment. Veterans of brutal combat environments may develop post-traumatic stress disorder. In both cases, it is not the person's fault that he or she was exposed to the situation which consequently affected behavior.

Laymen who think that mental illness is "all in the mind" and hence under voluntary control have missed the mark. No one is helped by blaming the disturbed person for his or her problems. An elementary understanding of the causes of behavioral disorder should convince everyone that pointing fingers is useless. This is not to say that the emotionally ill person is completely helpless and can exert no control at all. He or she may still be legally liable for personal actions and with help may be able to gain more control. However, merely telling someone to "snap out of it" or something similar will not undo the organic damage or functional loss of the person.

Types of Mental Illness

Psychopathologies run the gamut from relatively mild to quite severe. The milder forms are more common and more likely to appear in a library setting. Those individuals with more serious cases are likely to be institutionalized and will not appear in public as frequently.

Neuroses (Anxiety Disorders)

The various kinds of neuroses or anxiety disorders comprise the bulk of the milder mental illnesses. Neuroses are all characterized by the presence of abnormally intense or long-lasting anxiety. The mere presence of anxiety does not, of course, imply neurosis. Anyone facing a test, enduring an unpleasant job interview, or having a close brush with a major accident would justifiably experience some anxiety. Normal anxiety could even be intense and long-lasting, as long as the severity and duration were related realistically to actual stressors in the environment. For example, anxiety over a routine dental exam should be fairly brief and mild, while anxiety over a major and risky surgery might be strong and enduring. This is all normal. But what if the anxiety is out of all proportion to any actual stimulus in the environment? And, moreover, what if it begins to distort and even paralyze more and more of the person's ability to function? Such signs indicate neuroses. There are many types of neuroses.

Phobias. Phobias are extreme anxieties over specific objects or events. For instance, some people have extreme fears of heights, automobiles, or even being around other people. They eventually orient their lives around avoiding the stimuli which provoke the anxiety.

Obsessive-compulsive. Obsessive-compulsive reactions occur when people have odd thoughts (obsessions) or weird behaviors (compulsions) which they find irresistible. For instance, one library patron was constantly plagued by the thought that he might do himself or others harm. Another constantly wrote the same meaningless message on napkins, library slips, and various scraps of paper, producing dozens of copies each day and leaving them scattered all over the library. Such behaviors are manifestations of deeper underlying conflicts that the person feels incapable of facing.

Other anxiety disorders. These include such reactions as converting anxiety into bogus physical symptoms, perhaps of paralysis, blindness, or lack of feeling in the legs. These conditions must be distinguished from deliberate fakery on the one hand and actual organ damage due to stress, such as ulcers, on the other. For example, in *conversion reactions* the person thinks and acts as if damage has occurred, but it has not.

Personality Disorders

These involve disturbances in personality or interpersonal relations. For example, the psychopath or sociopath does whatever he or she wants regardless of the effects on others. Addictive personalities often turn compulsively to alcohol, drugs, or sex.

Adjustment and Impulse Control Disorders

Some patrons have trouble controlling their impulses and may repeatedly violate library rules or normal standards of decency. The kleptomaniac, for example, feels compelled to steal things, even things he doesn't really want or need, and these may include books and other items from the library.

Psychoses

Psychoses involve deep, serious breaks with reality and major breakdowns in behavioral functioning. The following personality types are among those suffering from psychoses.

Schizophrenics. These individuals have fragmented personalities out of touch with the reality around them. They may have weird ideas incomprehensibly expressed in splintered, often meaningless speech. For instance, with much careful listening you might catch on that they are trying to describe how aliens from spaceships have landed in the library and are disguising themselves as books; books with the letter "K" in the title indicate hidden aliens; these books must be destroyed at once to prevent an alien invasion. What distinguishes the schizophrenic from a mere prankster is that the former not only has some very odd, manifestly ridiculous ideas, but is incapable even of expressing them in a straightforward way. A schizophrenic's ideas and speech may constantly slip off focus, change direction, or degenerate into meaningless gibber. Further, his or her emotional reactions may bear no relationship to what is said.

Paranoids. These individuals often claim to be someone great or famous and usually maintain that others are out to get them. A paranoid may claim to be an actual famous person, perhaps Abraham Lincoln, or just some grandiose but fictional character, or perhaps the head of some mysterious spy agency that does not even exist. Such individuals are not merely pranksters and may be dangerous. Paranoids have a way of turning suspicious that others are pursuing them. For instance, the paranoid who thinks he is Lincoln may complain that one of the other patrons is John Wilkes Booth stalking him. The one who thinks he is a "super spy" may complain loudly and often to all who will listen that some of the library staff are enemy spies. Unlike schizophrenics, typical paranoids can express themselves well verbally. You can readily tell what their ideas are, but these notions have absolutely no bearing on reality. (These two separate patterns can also overlap in what is known as schizophrenia, paranoid type.)

Actual treatment of these conditions, of course, must be left to professionals. No library needs the liabilities inherent in a staffer trying to "play psychiatrist" no matter how noble his or her intentions may be.

Assessing Risk

Armed with an elementary understanding of the types of psychopathology most likely to appear in public places, library staff can begin to make reasonable assessments of the risks posed by such people.

Low Risk

Neurotics may be quite upset and could in a moment of panic accidently injure themselves. But they do not pose much risk to other patrons or staff except for being minor, but vexing, nuisances. The same is true for mentally deficient or retarded individuals, unless they have become agitated (perhaps by being teased or provoked).

Moderate Risk

Schizophrenics have a greater nuisance factor if they continue to insist their delusional ideas are true. They may get upset when confronted or challenged regarding the validity of their ideas. When upset, they may tend to lose self-control and could accidentally harm themselves or others. They generally do not, however, intend violence. The same is usually true of people with the lesser personality disorders, although when inebriated with alcohol or illegal drugs, they have more potential for violence in response to perceived threats.

High Risk

Paranoid people can definitely pose a high risk. The guy who thinks he is a "super spy" may decide to "get" the staffers he thinks are spies before they can get him. Psychopaths and others with severe personality disorders may also become dangerous, because they do not care or are incapable of caring about who gets hurt as they pursue their own desires. In both cases, there is a real threat, because the person will not respond realistically to the normal social forces which keep most people in line.

Knowing How to Respond

Naturally, the library staffer's response should be proportionate and related to the level of risk posed by the patron with a behavior disorder.

Low Risk

When dealing with a disturbed patron in the low risk category, there is no reason for concern. Try to calm and reassure the anxious patron and provide kind but firm guidance as to what the patron should do. The neurotic will usually respond to such social pressures. Higher authorities to help with the situation generally are unnecessary.

Moderate Risk

When confronted with patrons in this category, the employee should not act alone if possible. He or she should bring a co-worker or supervisor into the situation, both as a witness to the odd behavior and as back-up in case things turn worse. Do not humor the schizophrenic's delusions, but also do not remind him or her too strongly of reality. Stay calm and polite, directing the patron not to persist in telling you the story. Refer him to the police or to a mental health facility instead.

High Risk

Always consider a psychopath or paranoid to be dangerous even if he or she at times seems jocular or friendly. If alone when he expresses paranoid ideas of grandeur or persecution, do not contradict him or attempt to explain away his claims. He could work you into his delusion, deciding you are an enemy he must attack. Instead, try to keep him calm until further help can be obtained. Supervisors must be informed; also contact library guards or police.

Preparation, Confrontation, and Response

As indicated above, not all mentally ill patrons present problems. Some may be present in libraries regularly—perhaps even daily or over long periods of time—without creating disturbances or causing others fear or discomfort. If not presenting problems, these patrons should be allowed their rightful "use" of the facilities: if they request information or materials, they should be accorded the same respectful treatment and quality service as other patrons. This section addresses how to cope with those patrons whose behavior or presence in the library *has* become a problem.

Frequently, library "problem patrons" are individuals with some degree of mental illness. The woman shouting in the periodical room may seem, by her appearance, to be "merely homeless," but at least one third of the homeless are also mentally ill.[2] The man sleeping on the floor by the newspaper racks may seem to be "just a drunk." But about 40 percent of the homeless are also alcohol abusers,[3] and alcoholism has long been considered an illness.[4] Simply put, most "problem patron" encounters will involve individuals who are one—or a combination—of the following: mentally ill, homeless, or alcoholic. How to handle these situations is the focus of this chapter. (Chapter 1 of this book deals specifically with the homeless.)

It is important for librarians to distinguish between mentally ill patrons and those patrons who present service complaints or similar problems. Coping with other *confrontational* clients is presented in chapter 11.

The Coping Process

Problem patrons may appear in virtually any type of library: public, academic, institutional, corporate, and special. (Coping methods for academic libraries are suggested in chapter 6.) But due to ease of access alone, public libraries may encounter the greatest number of patrons with behavior problems. Public librarians, states a noted columnist, "are made to feel like baby-sitters, riot police, narcotics agents, social workers, and mental health specialists."[5]

Most library employees have seen problem patrons in library departments or branches, and many have been harassed or abused; some have been attacked and a few even killed.[6] But how many staff have actually *dealt* with problem patrons? And how many encounters have been successfully or properly handled?

For many librarians, dealing with problem patrons is like walking a tightrope—most are reluctant to try it and fearful of the outcome. It is a classic dilemma: staff and other patrons are angry if one does not respond. But if one *does* respond, there may be repercussions from supervisors for "handling it wrong" or from the perpetrator, who may become agitated, resentful, or even dangerous.

The following is testimony from a public library administrator who received nine death threats from one individual, three death threats from another, and was stalked for a time by a third. These patrons had all been barred from the library for disruptive behavior. The man who most likely phoned the nine death threats was a ***paranoid of the grandiose type*** (with delusions) with whom the administrator had dealt repeatedly during many months.

> This individual, who once told me he was actually the United States president, was huge—built like an NFL lineman (about 6′5″ and 240 pounds). I had received literally dozens of complaints from patrons and staff alike about his frightening and disruptive behavior. He stared at, argued with, and otherwise harassed staff. His noises, gestures, and brisk pacing were constant distractions. On occasion he even wore costumes or disguises like a surgeon's scrub uniform. He refused to respond to several informal warnings. In one formal conference he made veiled threats: (A) this was a "life and death situation for [him] and a life and death situation for [me]" and (B) "if [I] won't take care of this, [he has] friends who will take care of it for [him]." The complaints were so serious and numerous that we had no choice but to bar him; the library director informed him and I was present as a witness. Besides the two face-to-face threats, I soon began receiving phoned death threats at my office and home. Although the calls were anonymous, I had no doubt who initiated them. In the third phone threat, he specifically indicated that he knew where I parked (several blocks from the library) and when I got off work. One evening a few months later, I encountered him apparently waiting for me on my way to the parking lot, which was beyond some abandoned buildings and beneath a bridge. He was gesturing wildly and shouting in my direction . . . obviously very angry.

While retribution like this administrator experienced is rather extreme, some librarians find that angry patrons have smashed windows, slashed tires, egged houses, or perpetrated other vandalism. Of course, there are also cases of the unthinkable—deranged patrons actually attacking library workers and sometimes other patrons. It is important to realize, however, librarians are still responsible to other staff and patrons and *must* respond appropriately to problem situations. This book focuses on the practical aspects of how to deal with problem patrons: preparing (*paperwork* and *peoplework*), confronting (reacting and procedures), and the library response (determinations and documentation).

Preparing for Problem Patrons

The two major aspects of preparation for library problem patron situations are the *paperwork* and *peoplework*.

Paperwork

A very important part of the library's preparation is its policies (i.e., paperwork). Some libraries view this as a "security" policy, while others invoke labels like "Patron Behavior and Library Usage."[7] Whatever its designation, this document clarifies the library's purpose and indicates its general direction (such as restrictions versus guidelines, "tight" versus "loose"). The policymakers should try to determine the community's wishes to a certain extent. What are the community's trends? What is the library's social obligation? How will the policies affect the library's public relations?

Policy Content

The content of a good policy document will specify appropriate and inappropriate uses of the library, as well as unacceptable patron behavior. Most people would agree that appropriate uses of library facilities and materials include studying, researching, reading, writing, doing homework, tutoring, attending programs, and viewing exhibits. Good policies should also include inappropriate uses (like bathing, shaving, washing clothes, gambling, panhandling, and sleeping), as well as inappropriate behavior (for example, running, climbing, cursing, eating, and drinking). Many library policies even specify rules of attire such as required wearing of shoes and shirt.

The library's policy should focus on *items* which are not allowed, like animals and alcoholic beverages, rather than types or classes of people. Policies that prohibit items like bedrolls, blankets, large boxes, or plastic bags may represent thinly disguised discrimination against "drifters" or "vagrants." In addition to being socially irresponsible, that may be illegal in some places. The point is to prohibit specific types of behavior, not types of people. Policies should address patrons' behavior rather than their status. Libraries should not restrict or bar individuals solely because they look like "bums" or "weirdos." Besides, one often cannot tell by looks alone.[8]

Attempting to recognize the library's responsibility to staff and patrons, some policies rightly address such behavior as staring at people, following others, or leaving disturbing notes around the building. While certainly objectionable, these activities may or may not be illegal since their very nature makes them difficult to define or to prove. Check this and all other policy components with the library's governing body such as the city council for applicable laws and ordinances; cite appropriate guidelines in the policy. Be certain the library's board (or other authority) examines and specifically approves the policy and indicate the date approved. Find out whether the jurisdiction requires rules to be publicly displayed in order to be valid and enforceable.

Policy Format

The format of the library's policy statement should be clear and simple (perhaps in outline format). It should indicate appropriate and inappropriate uses and should list examples of behavior that are not allowed. Do not obscure the essence of the policy with legalese although the applicable ordinances could be appended. Administrators predisposed to complicated flow charts should remember that this policy may need to be consulted often by mid-level or low-level staff, in emergency situations at times. What is appropriate for training purposes may not be so helpful during emergencies.

Referrals

Some libraries may be able to mention referrals, such as food kitchens, somewhere in the policy. That may depend on what is available in that community, whether it is nearby, free, and able to provide the help typically needed by patrons. Questions to consider include: (1) how much staff time is involved? (2) do library employees have the expertise to discern the specific needs and select the appropriate agency? (3) is there any potential legal liability for giving such advice?

Challenges to Policies

These steps will help protect the library and its employees, but even the best policies can be challenged. Some complaints may be as simple as a demand to "show me that [rule or restriction] in writing" or the objection, "you don't have the right to [restrict me]." Of course, legal challenges can also be extreme. New Jersey's 1991 *Kreimer v.*

Morristown case went to a U.S. District Court, where the judge found for the plaintiff and ruled the library's policy was, in part, "unconstitutionally vague."[9] Nearly a year later, a federal appeals court panel reversed that decision, upholding the policy of Morristown Public Library. Libraries should keep the policy document separate from other policies (such as those for registration, circulation, overdues, fines, meeting rooms, and exhibit areas) because it addresses issues of potential danger.

Peoplework

Library administrators and supervisors must acknowledge that *paperwork* (policies) is practically useless without the *peoplework* (training) being emphasized. A wonderful example of good policies and good training is the widely reported 1994 incident at Salt Lake City Public Library. Patrons and staff escaped harm after a patron carrying a pistol and a homemade bomb held them hostage for several hours.[10] Quick thinking and calm reactions from staff contributed to the large facility's evacuation within five minutes. The gunman was shot by police while still in the library and died en route to a local hospital. The bomb was neutralized by police.

Training

If the library's policy is a revision of an existing one, at least distribute a memo explaining the differences and improvements. But if it is the library's first policy on dealing with patron problems, it should be properly introduced to the staff. This demonstrates to employees that they have the support—very important for those on the front lines—of the administration and the trustees. It may also help gain the confidence of the public regarding the safety of the library system or a particular branch.

The training or orientation session should include: (1) interpreting the policy, (2) applying it to current examples of actual situations in libraries, (3) answering employees' questions, and (4) role-playing, kept simple and brief. Discuss with employees the need to be alert and to watch for potential perpetrators. Explain to staff the importance of communicating with co-workers, leaving information for the next shift, and using discretion when discussing perpetrators.

Management Study

What are some of the management concerns regarding library safety? Look for situations with negative potential, for example, employees working alone in branches or departments and minimal staff coverage during lunches, breaks, shift changes, or closing time. Ask the staff to identify possible security problems, such as insufficient or inoperable lighting, isolated areas, corners hidden from view, too-high book stacks, poorly located restrooms, and remote parking lots. Ask employees for suggestions on desk arrangements, personal belongings, lockers, and staff lounge. Talk frankly with staff about being *ready* to call for police and *when* to call them if an incident becomes serious. Discuss the process of how to recognize when a situation is beyond staff's limitations and instruct them what to do in such cases.

Have someone investigate the cost and feasibility of buzzers, warning lights, "panic" buttons, or other alarms. Ask someone knowledgeable to examine the library's entrance and exit areas, as well as the streets leading there. Determine whether anything can be changed to increase safety for staff and patrons, particularly for those walking to and from cars after dark. Invite the local police department's crime prevention division to give a brief presentation to employees on precautions they can take at work and home, how to recognize the potential for dangerous situations, and how to avoid would-be perpetrators. Find out when police patrol the area around each library building and ask whether those patrols can be increased at certain times, such as at library closing, if necessary. Consider posting reminders for the patrons about protecting belongings since unattended purses and other valuables are easily expropriated in libraries.

Building Configuration

When building, re-building, or remodeling, be certain the main public service areas: (1) allow staff to have visual command of the environment, (2) minimize "hiding places," and (3) do not have "dead ends" in book stacks. Take a special look at the floor plans of offices, work areas, and small library branches to ensure people cannot come up behind staff unobserved. Whenever possible, provide two ways out of any spot in the library, so staff will not be trapped without an escape route. Even if no new construction is planned, grant permission for supervisors to rearrange a particular area so these issues are addressed.

Security Guards

Another aspect of *peoplework* preparation may involve security guards, though this tends to be expensive and is not often seen in smaller libraries. Of course, round-the-clock coverage is not the only option. Guards may be scheduled for the evening hours only, or during weekends when there are usually fewer staff. Some libraries regularly hire large young men (such as high school football players) as evening pages or desk workers in the hope that their presence dissuades would-be perpetrators. That may be an effective preventative, but the legal ramifications must be considered of having a *minor* (under age 21 in some states) involved in an actual dispute or confrontation.

Some libraries hire their own proprietary security and provide their own training, uniforms, and equipment. Such guards are typically more accountable to library personnel than guards provided by outside security services. Be sure to consider the hidden costs of background investigation of security personnel, supplemental liability insurance, licensing for guard training (if required), and whether or not weapons will be carried. Guard services usually take care of these matters, for a fee, of course. If using a security service, consider the quality of personnel they hire, how much above minimum wage they pay, and whether they are certified by a state or regional board, where applicable. Also, determine whether they are willing to cover brief shifts like 6 P.M. to 9 P.M. and if they schedule guards for shifts longer than twelve hours. Check the extensiveness of guard training, particularly if firearms are involved.

An off-duty or retired police officer may be an ideal solution to the logistics of uniforms, scheduling, and to the vexing issues of: (1) power of arrest, (2) firearms, and (3) liability. (Libraries deciding such issues independently of local police should definitely check the legality of those decisions.) However, using police as guards probably gives the library the least control over policy decisions and determinations about specific patrons or particular situations. This is usually the most expensive security arrangement.

Confronting Problem Patrons

To set the stage for confronting problem patrons, consider this occurrence one morning in a staff work area (on a non-public floor) of a public library headquarters downtown in a large city. Some employees mistakenly believe that problem patrons are indigenous only to the libraries' public service areas, and mainly in the evenings. They think perhaps they are protected by working in technical service or administrative areas in the daytime. Well, the following true example illustrates otherwise:

> I'm alone in a room with my back to the door while typing on a word processor; this man just appears out of nowhere. He's bald with irregular patches of hair and he smells horrible. He says, "I'm a CIA agent and I just need to know what I have to do to get food in the next three days." I'm completely off-guard and all I can think to say is, "I don't understand what you're asking me." To my surprise, he responds, "Okay, then I'll leave." And he

> does. I'm greatly relieved, but my adrenaline is still pumping and I'm thinking "that was too easy." But I write it up and distribute copies to the various departments and the security guard. Later in the afternoon, the same day, I'm alone in the same room (still typing) and I'm interrupted with a long distance phone call. Suddenly, I *smell* this guy! He appears again behind me. I turn around slowly, apprehensively, and ask him to wait in the hall while I finish my call. I'm hoping to get out of that room before he comes back and I end the call as quickly as I can. But just as I hang up, he comes back in, so he must have been waiting just outside the door. He comes quite close again and says he needs some help to "get [his] head straight." He has just now typed—downstairs on a terminal—that he's a CIA agent and wants to know if I've "received it yet up here." He's standing between me and the door and he blocks the only path between a large table and my work station. Hoping to get him out of my path, I slide a nearby chair toward him and slightly beyond the table. But he moves it *back* into the thruway and I realize I've just given up the only thing I had as a shield! He asks if I'm "with the government." He seems disoriented and confused, mumbles softly and incomprehensibly at times, and seems to struggle for what to say. He says he has "electrodes in [his] head" and has been "hooked up to Ted Turner." He's "patriotic," loves his country and wants a job. As if reading my mind, he says he does "not want to go to jail . . . or a hospital." He's rambling and repetitive, but doesn't DO anything actually threatening. Finally I look in the phone book for a local shelter; I write down the address and offer it to him. He concludes that wouldn't be a good place for him to go. Then, as in the morning encounter, he leaves peacefully, joined by the library guard who has evidently been waiting out in the hall. I'm left a bit rattled—and wondering why the guard didn't come *in* the room—but otherwise unharmed.

A Hollywood director couldn't make up anything stranger than that . . . and similar incidents occur practically every day in libraries of all types across the country. What do you do in cases like this? What do you say? How do you respond during encounters with individuals who are obviously mentally ill?

Reacting to Security Incidents

Problem patron incidents in libraries affect a lot of people besides those immediately involved. These individuals will have a variety of reactions which someone in the library must be prepared to handle.

What are some of the perpetrator's reactions? Many will deny their behavior, some will shout or curse, and others may go on the offensive, accusing staff or other patrons of misbehavior. Some individuals may resort to vandalism, violence, or assault. A good number of perpetrators, when confronted by an authority figure, may simply panic and, with luck, they will flee. Some, however, attack.

What are the reactions of other patrons who encounter such individuals in the library? Many are frightened or intimidated, and some will believe that the library is not safe and may never come back. It is likely that some will complain to the first librarian they see, or to the "head honcho," and demand that something be done to protect them. Remember, the staff must also deal with the patrons who may be fearful of mentally ill patrons.

What are the reactions of other staff? Some of them may panic while others may exhibit such physical symptoms as cold sweat, shaking, or quavering voice. A few will go on the defensive, which usually will not help and often makes the situation worse. Some, for fear of reprisal, such as a death threat, will actually pretend to ignore the misbehavior in the hope another employee responds. Some employees become frustrated or angry and a few may even resign. Occasionally, there are workers whose combination of compassion and moxie makes them excellent "managers" of such situations, and they will defuse or otherwise assist the patrons whose behavior cause problems in the library.

What are the reactions of supervisors or administrators? Some may be unaware of the problem, particularly if their offices are distant from the public areas. Other supervisors are aware, but literally hide or disappear from the problems. Many hope that avoidance will cover their fright or indecision. However, what kind of support does this indicate to the rest of the staff?

Who Reacts . . . and How?

Obviously, a library worker must analyze the situation and respond quickly. But who? There is no time for a conference and one cannot just flip a coin. Usually the responsibility for this should be that of the ranking (or senior) employee of the library department or branch involved. When possible, another staff member should be a witness but should not have to do or say anything. Presence alone can provide moral support and increase the safety factor. Those at the desk should be told where you are going and why and be ready to call the police if needed.

While proper reactions are very important, it is also possible to overreact. Consider the library security guard who, when approaching almost anyone exhibiting negative behavior, pulls out his chemical spray and holds it down by his side, within view of the patron. He considers it a precaution in case the confrontation turns negative, but that "readiness" undoubtedly will escalate more situations than it calms.

Confrontation Procedures

At some point it's evident that someone on staff must confront the individual whose behavior is disruptive, destructive, or dangerous. That is not an easy assignment and should not be undertaken too casually. Except for emergencies, when you must react immediately, most difficult library situations will allow some maneuvering room. This is the period of time when the respondent decides: (1) where to confront, (2) who or what to take along, (3) what to say, and (4) other related factors.

Where to Confront the Perpetrator

Where should the confrontation occur? As a general rule, select a location which is *neutral* (i.e., not an office), where you and the patron will be visible to other staff, and where possible disruption of other patrons will be minimal. As a safety precaution, select a site with at least two routes of egress: you do not want the patron to feel cornered, and you may need an escape.

What to Carry with You

What, if anything, should you take with you? Would you want a ruler or pair of scissors in your hands when confronting a problem patron? No. Why not? Both the ruler and the scissors could be interpreted by the patron or the public as weapons which certainly could escalate the situation. Furthermore, if taken from you by the patron, they could be used to harm you or others. Consider the legal ramifications of a library employee wielding a "weapon" against a patron.

Is it wise to carry something, or safe to carry nothing? That depends largely on the employee responding to the situation. The point of carrying anything is that having a "prop" gives you something to do with your hands, may provide a little edge of confidence, and can ease the tension of an encounter. With hands in pockets, you're more likely to lose balance if you have to move quickly, or it could slow your response if the patron "turns" on you. With hands behind the back, you could inadvertently give the impression (to the perpetrator) that you are hiding something . . . perhaps a weapon. With hands in front or at the sides, you may look particularly vulnerable which could send the wrong signal to the patron. Finally, if your hands are fidgeting or wringing, you'll likely appear nervous and *not* in control of the situation.

Personal favorites of this author are (1) a stiff notebook—the kind that holds a legal pad, (2) a clipboard—with the library's security policy on it, (3) a large, stiff holder—for current issues of display magazines, or (4) almost any PermaBound children's picture book. All of these items answer the objections: they won't be interpreted as weapons, they're logical items for a librarian to be carrying, and they give you something to do with your hands. Furthermore, all can be used defensively to deflect a jab or a blow if the patron becomes aggressive.

Put It in Words

It is important to have a definite determination in mind before approaching the patron since it is unwise to appear indecisive during the actual confrontation. But how do you express that? Think about this before you encounter the patron. Use your own style of speaking rather than sounding stilted or otherwise unnatural. Here are a few simple examples:

> "I have to ask you to leave. We've received complaints about the . . ."
>
> "If you can't be quiet (or stop . . .), you'll have to leave."
>
> "You've been officially barred from the library. If you come back, we'll call the police."

There are many useful sources for other examples.[11]

Other Do's and Don'ts

As the librarian approaches the problem patron, there are several things to monitor. Watch for sudden body movements, particularly the hands, and listen to what is being said. Look for suspicious bulges in a jacket or items hanging out of a pocket. Some experts advise you not to look the problem patron directly in the eyes; others suggest you do look at the eyes to better predict what he or she is about to do.

What do you do? Keep calm, approach slowly, speak in a low voice; be assertive, direct, and impersonal. There is no need to be aggressive or combative. Give the patron plenty of space, and try to keep something between you and him or her (such as a table, counter-high shelves, chair, or book truck). What *not* to do? Do not panic. Do not sneak up on or touch the individual. Don't say anything to agitate the perpetrator or do anything that is likely to escalate the situation. Don't threaten, argue with, or lie to the patron. Don't get emotional.

The Library's Response

At this point, we have reviewed how the appropriate policies should be produced and the staff trained. If the *confrontation* is what stops the problem behavior, the *determination* and discussion afterward will help prevent it from happening again. The administration or upper level supervisors should render determinations on each case to ensure that proper documentation regarding the situation is prepared.

Determinations

The same process by which library administrative decisions are made should be used to render determinations about many standard types of problem patrons (such as "drunks"). But what if the problem is a man who has been in the restroom screaming for ten minutes? It is impractical to leave that situation to call someone who confers with someone else. That's why many, or even most, determinations on problem patrons should be rendered by the floor supervisors, branch managers, or department heads who are on the scene. These supervisors would, of course, follow guidelines and policies already established by the administrators or boards. Libraries with security guards may leave such determinations to the guards themselves or possibly have the guard check with the senior librarian.

Types and Levels of Determinations

There are several types of determinations the library can invoke and they logically depend upon the seriousness of the patron's offenses. The lowest level is the *verbal warning*. Using simple, brief, and direct instructions that are delivered calmly and quietly, the librarian explains to the perpetrator what must change. For example: "you may not pound on the table" or "no alcohol is allowed in the library." When such minor offenses recur, some libraries will use numerical standards: for example, after two warnings, the next offense will result in expulsion.

Written warnings should be used sparingly. They usually are not any more effective than verbal ones and may leave the library with greater "exposure" to problems after the fact. However, a written warning might be appropriate when a patron's cumulative offenses are very distracting or aggravating, but no single incident in itself is really serious.

Expulsion is usually the next "higher" determination. This differs from barring (which follows) in that it restricts the patron from coming into the library for a specific time period, after which the patron may return to the library if the negative behavior can be controlled. Expulsion is usually best explained verbally and specifies how long, for example, one week or one month, the patron is expelled. Also, it must be explained that the behavior must not recur when the patron returns. The patron needs to be reminded of the expectations on the first day back.

Barring is usually the most severe library determination and is applied in cases of serious misbehavior such as threatening words or actions and sexual misconduct like "peeping" or "flashing." Generally, this is intended to be permanent, although some cases may be subject to later review. Depending upon the circumstances, the library administrator may decide to schedule a review after six months or a year. Other reviews may be requested by the barred patron or someone on that patron's behalf such as a relative, doctor, or lawyer. The review may result in the determination being upheld or circumstances may warrant giving the patron another chance.

Whether to have a problem patron arrested depends upon a number of factors: the seriousness of the offense, local laws, and who is involved in the confrontation. Some areas have laws regarding public drunkenness, disorderly conduct, assault, and so forth, which may be enforced by an arrest on the first instance. But laws regarding "entering and remaining" on the premises typically warrant an arrest only when the perpetrator violates a prior determination like barring or expulsion. Police are likely to ask a library worker to sign the charges, particularly if the perpetrator is being arrested for entering and remaining after being forbidden. The library respondent, or that employee's supervisor, should be prepared to do so. Without a signature, some police will simply release the perpetrator unless he or she is being arrested for an unrelated non-library charge. Enforcement of other laws such as for vandalism may depend partly upon the extent of the violation or the estimated value of the damage.

Application and Consistency

The library officials rendering determinations regarding specific behavior should try to balance the library's security concerns with the problem patron's individual needs. Some situations call for flexibility and compassion. For example, a patron who sincerely tries to cooperate with the library's rules of conduct might deserve an extra chance or two if his offenses are relatively minor. For some types of objectionable behavior, perhaps a referral for appropriate assistance should accompany an expulsion.

Determinations should be applied with reasonable consistency, though this is recognizably difficult in large facilities with several librarians or guards responding to disturbances. Two of the library's goals in its security program are to give perpetrators clear and firm guidelines of unacceptable behavior and to let other patrons know what conditions to expect, such as a safe environment. Determinations should not vary because of staff personalities: for example, one supervisor ignores certain behavior, another librarian gives only warnings, while a third employee usually expels problem patrons. Furthermore, determinations should not be affected by any extraneous perceptions of the perpetrator's sex, race, age, or socio-economic status (e.g., she looks poor, he seems homeless, that one's a drifter). Such differences in treatment would be unfair, unwise, and possibly illegal. As with policy matters and confrontation procedures, the application of determinations for problem patrons should be examined regarding their appropriateness and legality.

Documentation

The determination is certainly not the end of the library security process. It is very important to follow up with communication to staff, the trustees or commissioners, perhaps the police if they are involved, and even with the media or public if it is a serious incident. Since such follow-ups cannot and should not be handled only verbally, it is important to document the problem behavior, indicate how it was handled, and provide further instructions if necessary.

Components of Documentation

The documentation should briefly record the details of the actual incident, including time, date, and exact location. The amount of detail may depend on the seriousness and frequency of the offensive behavior and whether other patrons were involved or victimized. Normally, the employee(s) who witnessed it should write down, clearly and briefly, what happened, who handled it, and whether there were other witnesses. It should also be noted whether police were called and if the patron was arrested.

Usually problem patrons will not voluntarily give their names and staff does not have the legal authority to demand it or to search them for identification. Before checking library registration files or circulation transactions to obtain the name of a perpetrator, be certain that doing so does not violate any internal or external confidentiality policies. Sometimes there may be "clues" on such things as belts, jewelry, satchels, binders, or tatoos, but these may not necessarily be the individual's name. If police are involved, they can usually discover a name though sometimes it may be only an alias. A librarian should be able to get this information from them. Some patrons are known only by the nicknames staff have given them, but it is important to use discretion if committing these to paper. (This author recalls an uncomfortable experience trying to explain a nickname that was clearly visible on the paperwork to a problem patron during a review.)

Since the names of many problem patrons are not known, a complete description of the perpetrator is very important. As a minimum, this should include the patron's sex and race, any distinguishing physical characteristics such as facial hair, and apparel. Individual library employees may have different perspectives, depending upon their own height and weight, so some of their estimates may not be very useful. In such cases, staff should relate those data to known persons, for instance, "as tall as Jack," or "about my weight," or a fixed entity like the exit door frame. Estimates of the patron's age may also vary considerably due to circumstances such as alcoholism and homelessness, which usually make individuals look much older than they actually are.

While these aspects of documentation are normally recorded by the librarian, employee, or guard at the scene, the analysis is usually done by a supervisor or administrator. This is a higher level of documentation, which indicates such things as pattern of behavior, seriousness of the incident, and what determination was invoked. Also indicate here what steps to take and whether police should be called if the perpetrator reappears or misbehaves again.

Use of Documentation

Obviously, documentation that is not current or not properly distributed is relatively useless and may be viewed as not worth the effort. But documentation can be very helpful and important in making a library more secure for staff and patrons alike. Consider this example from a large public library headquarters:

> In one week, two female librarians, frightened but unharmed, were "grabbed" by a male patron, who fled the building on both occasions when the women resisted. The matter may have ended there except for the documentation. Weeks later, the perpetrator returned and an alert library worker phoned the administrator. One of the earlier victims pointed out the man and a department head indicated, "that's the same guy that pestered *Jane Doe*." Not wanting to risk falsely accusing anyone, the administrator consulted the security reports from the previous incidents. The description matched this man, so the administrator decided to bar him immediately, before any other employee or patron could be subjected to such possibly dangerous affronts. As the administrator approached, the perpetrator fled, but did not leave the building. Instead a chase ensued among the public service floors.

> Ultimately, the administrator informed the perpetrator he was barred and instructed him to leave immediately. The police were also called, but when they tried to question the perpetrator, he resisted and was wrestled to the ground. He had a knife concealed in his boot. Without documentation of the names and dates of earlier incidents, this patron possibly could have victimized several other women, particularly if he "struck" at various times and was seen by different staff. But with this documentation, the library had everything needed to press charges and assist the police.[12]

Documentation is also of value in court cases when the problem patron is brought to trial. At such times, the library's employees who dealt with the perpetrator may be subpoenaed as witnesses and called to testify. Months or years later it may not be easy without documentation to remember what the patron did, when and where it happened, or who witnessed it. Furthermore, good documentation will indicate if and when warnings were issued, what determination was invoked, and how the perpetrator violated it.

Summary

Every library should have a security policy to deal with problems posed by the mentally ill and others. It should be legal and appropriately adopted or approved. It should be understandable, easily accessible, and separate from other library policies. However, the policy is only as good as the training that accompanies it. Many potential situations can be prevented by good planning, careful placement, proper scheduling, appropriate contacts, coordination, training, and common sense. Preparation by the library staff should include the involvement of administrators, supervisors, and constant awareness on the part of employees. Buildings, branches, work areas, and offices should be designed to increase employees' field of vision, allow escape routes, and eliminate potential danger zones. Safety for employees and patrons should be emphasized at all times and information must be exchanged. Guards who are properly trained and scheduled can be effective deterrents to many would-be perpetrators.

When confronting a problem patron use common sense, observe the safety of staff and patrons, and take precautions. Respond quickly but don't overreact (or underreact); don't engage "solo" unless there is no choice. In most cases, carry something in your hands and use language that is clear, simple, short, and direct. Almost every aspect of these "rules of engagement" can be practiced in advance, such as by role-playing during a training session. The librarian's first confrontation is usually the most difficult.

Generally, documentation should be distributed quickly to the public service departments or branches with the notation that this information is *internal* and is being circulated for reasons of safety and security. Examples of various levels of documentation, which include format and detail, are available in a helpful source.[13]

Notes

1. Ellen Hale, "Care for Mentally Ill Still Abysmal, Report Concludes," *Shreveport Times,* Sept. 14, 1988, p. 1E.

2. "How Attempts to Help the Homeless Can Backfire," *U.S. News & World Report* 104 (Feb. 29, 1988): 33. From data in *Homelessness and Health* by James D. Wright and Eleanor Weber (Washington, D.C.: McGraw Hill's Healthcare Information Center, 1987).

3. Ibid.

4. American Psychiatric Association, *Diagnostic and Statistical Manual of Mental Disorders,* 3rd ed., rev. (Washington, D.C.: American Psychiatric Association, 1987). Sample "classifications" as per DSM-III-R: alcohol intoxication (303.00), alcohol dependence (303.90), alcohol abuse (305.00), and "dementia associated with alcoholism" (291.20).

5. Will Manley, "Facing the Public," *Wilson Library Bulletin* 64 (Feb. 1990): 61.

6. "Patron Fatally Wounds Librarians in Sacramento," *Library Hotline* 22 (April 26, 1993): 1.

7. "Guidelines for the Development of Policies regarding Patron Behavior and Library Usage," *Library Journal* 117 (March 1, 1992): 51.

8. Jon Kartman, "Seattle PL Receives [$100,000] from Smelly 'Fish Man,'" *American Libraries* 23 (Sept. 1992): 619.

9. "Appeals Panel Upholds Morristown's Policy," *Wilson Library Bulletin* 66 (May 1992): 13.

10. "Bomber Holds Librarian and Patrons Hostage at Utah PL," *Library Journal* 119 (April 1, 1994): 17.

11. Charles A. Salter and Jeffrey L. Salter, *On the Frontlines: Coping with the Library's Problem Patrons* (Englewood, Colo.: Libraries Unlimited, 1988), 133–34.

12. Ibid., 73–77.

13. Ibid., 155–60.

3

Opposites Attract: Young Adults and Libraries

Patrick Jones

A public library story time concludes and preschoolers begin running around the place yelling like mad, and it is deemed acceptable behavior. Two senior citizens loudly discuss their medical bills while standing at the copier, and no staff member asks them to be quiet or to move. A "regular" patron's winded and full-voiced discussion of the latest best-seller is accepted. Or a group of six adults, having left a library program, stand directly in front of the circulation desk discussing the program and no one says anything to them. But at 2:30 P.M., two young adults enter the building talking and laughing, which is somehow the end of the library world as we know it, and their entry prompts the classic "shhhh" response from the nearest library employee. Some young adults just laugh it off, some ignore it, and some just turn around and leave, wondering what *our* problem is.

Libraries and library staff seem to be gunning for young adults, and the young adults know it. At the same time, many librarians think that the sole goal of many young adults is to disrupt the quiet of a peaceful library setting. Both assumptions are basically wrong but follow logically, given the contrasts between young adults and libraries.

Young adults are loud and libraries are quiet, and, well, opposites do seem to attract. If a list were compiled of all the stereotypical characteristics of young adults and matched with a list of how young adults view libraries and librarians, the contradictions would be apparent. The things librarians often value—organization, quiet, reflection, civility, and love of the printed word—is contrasted with the stereotypical young adult traits of disorder, loudness, constant motion, rudeness, and the love of the *image*. Yet despite the apparent divisions between librarians and young adults, bridges can be built and connections made in many instances.

The focus in this chapter is on what to do when young adults pose problems and how to develop strategies to correct inappropriate behavior, which often ensues when young adults congregate in libraries. (Issues like youth gangs are not young adult problems, but rather a problem of criminal behavior in the library. The library cannot solve the gang problem which is an issue for the community, not just the library.) Our concern is more about gangs of young adults as opposed to young adults in gangs.

Why Young Adults Come to the Library

Young adults congregate in libraries for a variety of reasons. The most obvious reason is the same reason others do—because they have an information need which the library can meet. Sometimes this information need is school-related and at other times it is not. For a lot of young adults, the home is not the right place to study and the library is the obvious alternative. For younger teens, libraries are places where they feel comfortable, in a world they are more confused about daily. Regardless of their motives, young adults need libraries and libraries need young adults.

Libraries also serve as an after-school social center for young adults. In many communities, when school is over there is no place available for young adults to gather except local public libraries. The library is free, easily accessible, and known. It is also an acceptable place for parents to send young adults since libraries are viewed as safe havens. Libraries also meet the needs of latchkey, homeless, or runaway young adults. Finally, young adults know that unlike fast food outlets, parking lots, or other temporary gathering places, libraries often have a high tolerance level for a group of young adults.

The Problems They Pose

It is the "congregation" aspect—the wolf pack image—that causes the most problems for libraries. When young adults gather, problems may occur. In some libraries, it is just a numbers problem. For those libraries located near schools, the crowd which gathers after 2:30 can be intimidating for no other reason than its sheer size. This scenario requires real leadership from staff: A sole young adult librarian is not the answer to serving seventy-five young adults at once. The person in charge of the library must set the tone and develop the strategy for all staff.

If during this time library staff are merely acting as security guards, then a better use of library resources would be to hire a security guard rather than using staff. Instead, staff should be working with schools to develop alternative after-school programs, working within the community to find recreational alternatives and, finally, training library staff on how to tolerate young adults.

If a group of seventy-five adults, preschoolers, or even library staff all converged in the library at one time, there would be noise and disturbance. Developing realistic expectations of young adult behavior is the first step to solving the young adult patron challenge.

Part of the problem is contrasting energy levels. Most libraries are rather passive places and when a group of young adults enters, the energy level shoots up. The young adult years are a time of excessive energy, marked by confusion, lots of physical activity, a lack of perspective, and the need for social interaction and personal attention.

Why They Can Pose Problems

Young adults behave the way they do because of pressure from the constant changes they are experiencing. Not yet adults, but not wanting to be considered children, young adults often feel like confused, caged animals. Consequently they may lash back at society in their confusion, insecurity, and loneliness. Add to that the fact that many young adults are in libraries to complete an assignment they resent or are there due to boredom and looking for entertainment.

The physical, emotional, and social changes that young adults experience are called *developmental tasks.* The primary developmental tasks of young adults are:

1. Physical activity
2. Competence and achievement
3. Self-definition
4. Creative expression
5. Need for positive interaction with peers and adults
6. Need for structure and limits
7. Desire for meaningful participation

Understanding each of these developmental tasks helps increase understanding of why young adults are often perceived as problem patrons in libraries.

For example, consider the task related to physical activity. Sometimes young adults have too much energy for libraries where the ground rules are basically "sit down" and "shut up." Neither of these rules are easy to follow, especially when many young adults visit libraries after a full day of "sit down" and "shut up" confinement at school. After a day of school with its rigid rules, it is no wonder that young adults who make the exodus to public libraries are talkative and easily excitable: the cap has been on the bottle all day. Libraries are not places for physical activity, but young adult areas in public libraries can often help by containing this energy in one area. The best method for crowd control is to at least contain the crowd in one location where behavior can be more easily monitored and modified.

Understanding the developmental tasks for young adults on structure and limits is the key to correcting problem behavior. Young adults are in a day-to-day learning process regarding acceptance of responsibility. They have been told what to do as children, but now are faced with choices with little clarity on the limits of their choices. Thus, they test the limits or boundaries. Foul language, outrageous clothing, loud and rebellious music, code-word slang, and other behaviors are all related to limit testing. Confrontations between librarians and young adults often revolve around this very issue: how much is allowed and who decides the limits. Understanding this task explains the contempt young adults may have for adults, especially those connected with institutions like libraries. It explains why some young adults are constantly talking back and challenging. Finally, it explains why librarians should always correct inappropriate behavior ("these are the limits and you have passed them") rather than the person. Think about how you would like to be corrected when you are learning a new job or task. Do you want to be attacked and made to feel stupid, or do you want to learn from your mistakes and how to do better? This is what young adults are experiencing daily, learning how to be a responsible person in society.

Remembering this abstract concept is difficult when confronted with a group of boys cursing loudly in the reference area, or a group of girls shouting at each other in front of the library's front door. In both cases, it is clear that the behavior is inappropriate, not because it is loud, but because it disrupts others using or staffing the library. This is the litmus test—does the behavior disrupt others? If a class is supposed to be doing homework, yet several boys are passing around the *Sports Illustrated* swimsuit issue, then although annoying, the behavior is not inappropriate because it does not disrupt others. Or if groups of young adults come during the evening, plop down their textbooks, and then proceed to spend three hours gossiping and giggling quietly, that is not disruptive either. What a young adult does in a library is his or her own business, unless it disrupts others or is against the law. The real question for young adults and librarians is: "who has the problem here?" Clearly, when young adults are talking but not disrupting others, the problem is *staff reaction,* not young adult action.

The matter is one of going beyond stereotypes and playing fair. Librarians have no right to tell young adults to "get back to work" or ask "shouldn't you be studying?" We certainly would never think of monitoring adult patrons' activities in such a way. Similarly, some libraries post signs stating "no more than two students at a table" or "no students during school hours without a pass." Would the same libraries post signs not allowing more than two African Americans at a table or stating that no business people are allowed in the library before 3:00 P.M. without a note from their boss? Of course not, yet these clearly discriminatory prohibitions are in place in some public libraries. Such responses speak only to the stereotypes of young adult behavior, not to its reality.

How to Deal with Disruptive Behavior

The question is how to deal with the reality of disruptive behavior among young adults. In addition to understanding why some young adults behave as they do, several strategies are in order. These strategies are based on the five library "r's": relationships, rules, reactions, and responsibilities, with the final "r" being the most basic and important of all—respect. Some librarians just do not *like* young adults, and no matter what is written here or anywhere else, that is not going to change. No one can require librarians to like the people they serve, but respect can be required. The key is respecting young adults as library patrons. Rather than characterizing all of them as "loud kids" or defining them as the "young adult problem," librarians must view young adults as patrons who demand, require, and deserve our respect. If they are not viewed in this manner, then librarians may actually be the disruptive element, not the young adults.

Relationships with Young Adults

It is important to identify the groups of young adults and their leaders. Staff energies should be directed toward meeting the leaders—getting to know their names, their likes and dislikes. It is important that the leader work with you and not against you, which can contribute to the peer group policing itself to keep things cool.

More importantly, librarians need to establish a relationship with young adults other than that of acting the role of the "quiet police." If that is the young adults' only image of a librarian, then the only role they can play is the one that challenges authority. But what if they saw the librarian in a different role, such as the person who came to their classroom to discuss books and library materials, or the one who showed them how to use the library to complete a report? Maybe then they would believe that someone at the library is interested in their needs. Young adults could define their relationship with the library differently when there is a familiar staff face or name.

Relationships with Staff

No one staff person can solve problems that occur with young adults, so everyone on staff has to be committed to solving such problems. All staff, not just young adult librarians or others who serve young adults, need to be informed and educated about youth behavior. It is pointless for a young adult librarian to work hard to improve relationships with young adults if the clerk at the checkout desk is rude and insulting to them. Not everyone on staff will be a young adult advocate, but everyone must understand that young adults are patrons first, just as others are who use the library.

Relationships outside the Library

Find out what other groups in the community serve young adults. Network with schools, youth groups, churches, human service agencies, and whomever else in the community works with young adults. Join or help form a youth service coalition. Try to work with the chamber of commerce or businesses which also cater to teens and may face some of the same problems.

Also, a working relationship with the police department is essential. Sometimes young adults may get out of hand and staff may need the help of police. Consider your expectations. Does the library want the police to simply show their badges, or is it willing to take action against patrons who might engage in criminal behavior, including trespassing? Do not ever threaten to call the police, just do it. Bluffing young adults is the wrong game to play, because it is just another limit they can test.

If disruptive patrons refuse to correct the behavior after reasonable efforts by library staff, then this is no longer a library problem, but perhaps a criminal one to be handled by professionals trained to deal with such matters.

Your Self-Esteem

It is important to be self-confident when dealing with young adults. They may call you names, bait you, and try to make you feel lousy. It takes a degree of toughness to deal with some young adults, even if there is an understanding of why they do certain things. If they cut you down, it is probably just to make themselves feel bigger, which is what they are often trying to do. Remember, self-esteem is a young adult's *daily* concern.

Unwritten Rules

The one problem with written rules of behavior is they are open to interpretation and, with young adults, the rules often invite challenge. A simple posted rule, "no gum allowed," seems clear, but young adults can heatedly engage you for minutes with retorts of "it says no gum, not no chewing gum" or "it says nothing about chewing tobacco." It may seem safer to have written rules of conduct. However, unless young adults are active in developing the rules, the rules may cause more problems than they prevent.

Noise versus Disruptive Behavior

Even with no posted rules for use of the library, there is one overriding rule that applies to everyone: if a behavior disrupts others, then that behavior is inappropriate and must cease or that person may be asked to leave the building. This is simple enough but sometimes unclear to young adults who tend to get carried away. A small group studying quietly can get loud very quickly. But are they consistently disruptive? Probably not, although things may have been out of control for a moment. The hardest thing is to know when a group is indeed going to get out of control. If possible, maintain eye contact with the perceived leader at the table, which might help control the situation.

Be Fair, Firm, and Consistent

The honor students should not be treated differently from the ones that take shop classes; in the young adult world there is no playing favorites. Approaches to young adults must be firm. Do not meekly suggest, "Gee whiz, can you please not be so loud?" Rather, make a firm statement that their behavior is inappropriate and cannot continue. Finally, as mentioned earlier, this must be as consistent as possible among all staff members.

The rules cannot change from day-to-day because that confuses young adults and can create problems for everyone.

What has been unsaid pertains to the gender problem. Librarianship is a female-dominated profession, and the job of being a young adult hell-raiser is a male-dominated one. Another contradiction and obstacle is that in many libraries it is also a race or ethnic issue. Because of this, some additional training from outside the library world may help staff better handle situations where there are some not-so-hidden agendas or challenges. Male librarians do not get paid extra to "act the heavy" and should not be expected to do so.

Enforce Rules

Staff need to be serious about enforcing rules. Do not threaten to throw young adults out eight or nine times without doing it, or just ignore them and hope they will go away. If staff members are going to intervene, it must be prepared to follow through. If the behavior continues, then staff must be prepared to seek assistance to enforce the rules. If young adults realize a person is all bark and no bite, then they will continue to taunt. If a particular young adult is a constant problem, then do not allow him or her back until the behavior changes.

Work with the library board to develop mechanisms for prohibiting individuals who are consistently disruptive in their behavior from the library. With young adults, if that person is a negative-examples peer leader, then the very best thing to do for all young adult patrons is to rid the library of that person. Whatever baggage or garbage that person might have, you are not going to resolve it. It is unfortunate to "write off" a young adult when probably everyone else has, but it is not the staff's job to save the world or that one young adult. If the goal is to make a better environment for all young adults and to give staff a positive image of this age group, then ridding the library of a constant negative influence seems advisable.

Don't Escalate the Problem

In enforcing the rules, remember that young adults will often challenge them. They will want to ask questions or say things like, "it is a public library, so I'm allowed here." Without being totally obnoxious, staff merely needs to restate the position: "correct the behavior or leave." Further discussion often leads to debates which may lead to shouting matches. In addition to a nasty scene in front of other patrons, if the young adults "get to you," then they may try to do so again. One probably cannot avoid confrontations, but there are ways to derail heated conflict.

Don't Power Trip

Librarians actually have a lot of power over young adults. However, a simple slash mark on the daily tally of questions might be perceived as a life or death matter to many young adults. One reason librarians have a bad image with young adults is that they often see librarians as mean and controlling persons, who view the library as their own when it really belongs to the public, including young adults.

This power can also manifest itself in trying to control problem situations. If you abuse your power, then you are setting up a dangerous situation. If you humiliate, embarrass, or humble a young adult, that person will remember it, probably for a long time. In this case, in winning you have really lost by losing the respect of the other young adults and perhaps some self-respect as well.

Keep Cool

As mentioned, young adults delight in the shock value of their actions. If you get angry, then they "win." It is really about limit testing, trying to get a reaction from you. If you lose your cool or get rattled, it is just the reaction they want and the "payoff" for their inappropriate behavior. Appropriate response is hard, but try to just let things bounce off. They will test you like they would test a new teacher or a substitute at school.

It Is Not Personal

Remember, it is not a personal thing if they call you a name, because they feel a need to test or maybe to strike out at an authority figure, not you personally. So expect to be called names, to have physical flaws and imperfections pointed out, clothing choices to be trashed, and just about every single part of your person attacked. Realize it really has nothing to do with you.

Lighten Up

Young adults make mistakes because they are young adults learning this job known as life. Most of these mistakes are not the end of the world (or even the Dewey Decimal System). If we constantly overreact to everything, then real connections are hard to make. All that stress we feel so often from working with young adults is not always from them, but from ourselves. Again, developing realistic expectations regarding young adult behavior is the key.

Project and Remember

Before we react to a young adult, we should take a moment to remember being a young adult. If we could summon up all those feelings of insecurity and confusion, and then project them on that young adult who is causing us a problem we may be more understanding. Those young adults are going through the same sorts of emotions as we did once. If librarians could remember and empathize with them, our reactions would be more satisfying to both groups.

The Choice of the Young Adult

Staff can put the onus on the young adult or young adults behaving inappropriately, making it their choice: "Look, your behavior is inappropriate, because it is disrupting others. If you choose to behave this way, then you are choosing to leave. If you wish to stay, then you must be less disruptive. You decide."

The Staff

As discussed earlier, part of *every* library staffer's job is to handle situations correctly. This is not solely the responsibility of the young adult librarian.

The Group

Also as discussed earlier, the peer group is the most important force in young adult life. Try to get young adults to develop their own methods of policing behavior. Tell the peer leader that if the group continues to be disruptive then everyone leaves. Use the peer group to your advantage.

Community

Young adults who hang out at the library and cause trouble often do so because they are bored and there are no other alternatives. This is not only a library problem but a community problem. Sometimes the biggest young adult problem facing libraries is the sheer number of young adults in too small a space during a certain period of time. If the library is being used by these hoards of young adults as an activity center rather than as a library, then it is the library that should be working within the community to see that the community becomes responsible for its youth.

Society

We need to value our young adults if we value our society's future. None of the strategies discussed earlier is foolproof. Like all problem patron situations, solving these problems takes a large dose of good judgment, timing, and people skills.

It might be difficult for some people to think that young adults deserve respect, but the fact is that the minute a young adult walks through the door of a library, he or she becomes a library patron deserving respect. Librarians and young adults might be opposites in many ways, but we do share the same space and should learn to live with each other.

4

Older Adults: Problems and Needs

Linda Marie Golian and Linda Lou Wiler

Library staff who use a proactive service perspective rarely perceive older adult patrons as problematic. An enlightened library staff realizes that ignoring the special needs of older adult users quickly results in frustrated, problematic older adult patrons. They discredit artificial distinctions between the elderly and other patrons, and, instead, anticipate the visual, auditory, physical, access, and computer technology limitations. Effective library staff members recognize the diversity of older adults and provide needed and desired materials. They adopt an earnest philosophy of caring about patrons and strive to create a win-win situation for the library and the older adult patron.

Society traditionally defines older adults as people age 65 and older. Historically, library staff members have viewed these users as difficult and problematic patrons. However, today's effective library administrators consider the physical and emotional changes in older adults and encourage enlightened and proactive service. They note how visual, auditory, physical, access, and technology limitations frustrate older patrons. Allowing for these limitations, library visionaries include the varied intellectual needs of this diverse group in their planning. Library staff members who strive to understand and anticipate these special needs rarely consider older adults as problematic patrons.

Background

The elderly comprise an ever increasing proportion of the American population. Statistics reveal that between 1980 and 1990, the elderly population grew by 22 percent, from 25.5 to 31.2 million. Projections show that America's elderly population will continue to grow dramatically through the middle of the twenty-first century, increasing by an estimated 19 percent, for a total of 99.5 million older adults by the year 2050.[1]

Stereotyping any population group creates many problems. Library staff members must understand the special needs of older patrons while recognizing the elderly as a diverse population group. Statistics reveal a future filled with an even greater racial and multicultural variance in this group.

Today's older adult patron is different from those of earlier years. Traditionally, aging meant retirement, decline, disease, frailty, and death. This view is changing to one of health, intellectual growth, and increased potential. Many older adults have a wealth of experiences and talents, along with the energy and adaptability needed to put them to work. Today's views must continue to change as tomorrow's older adult patrons become a generation with unique characteristics.

Despite these changes, many library planners continue to provide weak or inadequate services and programs for this very special population. Some library officials expect older patrons to adapt to materials, services, and programs established for traditional library patrons. While some older adults do fit into traditional programs, many do not. Librarians often ignore the special visual, auditory, physical, access, and computer needs of older patrons. These actions foster a troubled and sometimes hostile atmosphere which causes many library staff members to perceive older adults as problem patrons.

Serving Older Patrons with Visual Difficulties

America is a sight-centered society where library services and programs traditionally revolve around printed materials or other materials meant for viewing. This fact causes problems because failing eyesight is a basic medical symptom affecting most older adults. Broadly defined, ***visual impairment*** is difficulty in seeing even with corrective lenses. Visual difficulties create life adjustment problems for older adults, especially if reading has been an important part of their lives.[2]

Visual problems prevent many patrons from fully enjoying their library's programs and collections.[3] Library staff must realize that age affects vision and decreases reading speeds in older patrons. To help ease the frustrations that might be misdirected toward the staff, loan policies could be lengthened. Increased lighting is another answer to this problem. Even in new buildings with state-of-the-art lighting, it is not unusual to hear comments such as "How can you see in here? The light is so dim." One reason for this comment is that older eyes take longer to adjust from the harsh glare of the outdoors to indoor illumination.

Libraries can prevent many visual complaints by creating ample reading areas with generous, non-glare, lighting. Installation of additional fluorescent lighting is one recommended option. Whatever the artificial lighting source, it is crucial that library staff fix flickering lights promptly. Another solution is the creation of reading areas near skylights and windows, because modified natural lighting provides excellent illumination.

When increasing lighting, place careful consideration on reducing glare. Scattered light is the primary cause of glare. To avoid this condition, experts suggest using lighting that has a yellow rather than a blue hue.[4] Library material selectors also should consider creating and selecting reading materials on non-glossy paper.

Many older adults have impaired depth and peripheral vision. To help these patrons, library staff need to present information directly within the visual field of the sight-impaired individual. Materials posted too far to the left or right of the viewing area are rarely noticed. Posters and signs should hang at eye level for easier viewing by patrons wearing bifocal glasses. Additional suggestions to follow for easing sight problems for older patrons include preparing all handouts in large and boldfaced type, creating signs with large diagrams and sharp color contrasts, and providing magnifying lenses.[5]

Serving Older Patrons with Hearing Impairments

Like vision, hearing is a crucial communication link in our society. Older adults often suffer from a progressive decrease in their auditory threshold, characterized by an inability to distinguish sounds. Many older adults have difficulty differentiating conversations from background noise. This is one reason some older patrons complain about a noisy library environment during special events or even about prolonged quiet private conversations.

The most common type of hearing loss in aging is *presbycusis.* Presbycusis is the inability to hear either high or low pitch sounds.[6] A frequent cause of this common hearing loss is long-term exposure to excessive noise, commonly called noise pollution. Many older adults with this hearing problem use hearing aids. Ill-fitting hearing aids with weak batteries often whistle. It is not unusual for this noise to disrupt the reading, research, or study of fellow library patrons. In these situations library staff must tactfully approach and advise the older adult of the problem.

Auditory difficulties also negatively affect information processing. Thus, many older adults require additional time to process auditory information. Some adults with hearing difficulties become frustrated because they must work harder and longer to process everyday information.[7] In addition, many adults with hearing difficulties are reluctant to acknowledge auditory problems. In such cases, older patrons may accuse the library staff of deliberately mumbling to them.

Helping older patrons with hearing difficulties requires a conscious effort to ensure comprehension of verbal communications. Suggested methods for improving communication with persons with hearing difficulties include speaking clearly, avoiding a monotone voice, repeating important facts, and using visual aids. Providing written documentation for commonly asked questions and frequently requested information also anticipates and alleviates many problems.

It is helpful to create an environment free from distracting sounds. Libraries should install carpet and various wall treatments to help reduce noise. Many older patrons fondly remember the library as a quiet sanctum. This may require the library staff to patiently explain the change in library philosophy: the library is no longer a place where the librarian is continually asking the patrons to be quiet, but a place of communal learning.

Serving Older Patrons with Physical Problems

In today's fast-paced world, many people are impatient with slow-moving individuals. Researchers speculate that the slower pace of many older adults is a major cause for age discrimination.[8] Older library patrons face reductions in both reflex and reaction time. For them, simple tasks like picking up a book might be impossible because of health and aging complications.[9] The resulting slower pace of most older adults creates the view that they are out-of-sync with the rest of society.

Library staff members need to realize that the natural physiological changes of aging eventually affect all aspects of a patron's life. Aging influences everything from bodily control to flexibility and strength. A lack of bodily control may be one reason a patron complains "It sure stinks in here." In this circumstance, it is not uncommon for library staff members to have to address the sanitary needs of incontinent patrons.

Librarians have a responsibility to foster a supportive and patient attitude when working with older patrons. Most older adults, given ample time, can perform physical and mental library tasks as well as younger people. Sensitivity training for all library staff is an effective means for furthering true understanding of older adults. Effective training includes concrete guidelines that every staff member can easily follow. This training should help library staff recognize that many older patrons require additional time to move about physically in the library.

One simple sensitivity exercise requires a roll of gauze, medical tape, cotton balls, and a few sticks. The goal of this exercise is to help the staff understand the various disabilities of older adult patrons. For a brief period, immobilize staff members by taping two fingers together, stuffing their ears with cotton, splinting a knee, and covering their eyes with a thin piece of gauze.

This exercise helps library staff understand why some older patrons ask for help in retrieving library materials. Some older patrons just do not have the physical energy to retrieve the materials themselves. Others are physically and psychologically unable to reach for materials on high shelving for fear of falling books. Many older adults have physical difficulty grabbing and holding onto materials.

Library administrators also can help patrons with physical limitations by purchasing reading chairs with arms to enable older adults to push themselves up and out of the sitting position. Libraries also should install ramps and grip bars throughout the library, especially in the rest rooms.[10]

Serving Older Patrons with Access Limitations

Older adults are more likely to use the library when they have both a need and easy access.[11] Many older patrons are not able to get to the library whenever they wish. Lack of transportation and health restrictions are the two primary factors causing this limitation.

Older adults lose several transportation options during the aging process. Many individuals no longer feel comfortable driving a car. Some have lost a significant other who was their primary driver. Others live in communities with inadequate or no public transportation options. As a result, many older adults begin to depend upon their family and friends for transportation. Finally, when compared with grocery shopping, banking, and doctor appointments, visiting the library becomes a less essential transportation priority.

Health restrictions also limit library access for older adults. Many infirm elderly are physically restricted to their homes, hospitals, or short-term health care centers. Some older frail adults spend their days in senior citizen centers or adult day-care facilities. Unless the library comes to them, they are unable to use the library's exceptional services.

To meet the special access needs of older patrons, library administrators should strategically review their outreach programs. They need to question if their books-by-mail and bookmobile services are effectively reaching their community's older adult patron population. Improving services to these special patrons might include expanding and coordinating a books-by-mail program with local hospitals and health care facilities. Library staff can try to obtain the names and addresses of patients wishing to participate in this program before they begin extensive homebound recovery. Library administrators also can make an effort to provide bookmobile services and special service programs to local area retirement centers and adult day-care facilities.

Libraries can help older adult patrons by reviewing their library loaning policies. As with the visually impaired, many older adults with access limitations find it helpful to have longer loan periods. They also benefit from fewer restrictions on the number of library materials they can borrow at one time and the ability to renew materials by telephone.

Helping Older Patrons Deal with Current Technologies

Traditional societies viewed older adults as the repositories of knowledge and the transmitters of culture, customs, and history. Unfortunately, in our current technological society, older adults have lost most of that function.[12]

To assist older adults in regaining the dignity of their traditional role, library administrators need to recognize false stereotypes. This includes recognizing unwarranted assumptions concerning older adults and their attitudes toward information technology and change. Actually, most older adults usually are eager to learn new technologies. They want to feel connected to society and realize information technology helps them bridge an important gap. Learning to use new information technology allows them to stay busy and involved.[13]

It is not technological resistance, but physical limitations such as fatigue, failing eyesight, and lessened manual dexterity that often cause older adults to reject new technologies.[14] For these reasons, the complaint, "I have lived ninety years without a computer so why should I use one now!" is not uncommon.

Librarians have an obligation to learn how to adapt information technologies to the physical and learning limitations of older adults. To aid older patrons, library administrators should create computer user areas where older adults can sit, rather than stand. They should investigate using touch screen menus, delay keys, and dispensing glare screens, and wheelchair access should be provided. Library directors also should invest equipment funds to purchase one or two large screen monitors and provide paper printouts for adults with visual difficulties.[15]

Additional Concerns regarding Older Patrons

Acknowledging the special visual, hearing, physical, access, and technology concerns of older adult patrons is only the first step for providing essential and effective library services. The manner in which libraries acknowledge and address older adult needs is also crucial. Besides understanding these special physical needs, library staff members must strive to provide patron services in a compassionate, realistic, respectful, and professional manner.

Older adult patrons are similar to other library users in their diversity and temperament. It is important to remember that a nasty 70-year-old patron was probably once a nasty 25-year-old patron. Library administrators need to help their staff realize that negative comments made by older patrons should not be taken personally. It is not unusual for library staff to serve the occasional cranky older gentleman who demands that the library meet his needs right now! After all, he exclaims, "I'm a war veteran, and taxpayer, and ought to have some privileges!" Individuals like this are no different from younger demanding patrons and should be treated with the same firmness and the same diplomacy.

Just as some patrons are very vocal, others have difficulty verbalizing their needs. Some older patrons expect library staff members to "read their minds" and provide services without any conversation or verbal request. They quietly slip like a shadow into a library chair and expect the staff to come and serve their needs.

An atmosphere of genuine concern about patrons should pervade the library. To accomplish this ambience, staff members must practice patience and good listening skills. They should treat older patrons with respect and dignity. Library staff must realize that a loss of hearing, vision, physical movement, mental quickness, or bladder control does not indicate a loss of intelligence. Materials and services that fulfill the intellectual needs and desires of older patrons must be provided.

Library staff members have an obligation to build bridges that allow older adults continuing opportunities to use and enjoy library facilities and materials. To accomplish this task, they must actively anticipate the needs of older patrons, before the older adult becomes a problem patron. Library staff should not be surprised or act negatively when hearing such comments as: "Don't I get a discount on fines? I'm over sixty-five!" or "What do you mean I have to wait for that reserve book. I'm eighty-seven years old and don't have the time to wait." Each age group thinks that it is special. Anticipating these attitudes will help mitigate many problems.

Materials for Older Adults

Physical improvements, attitude changes, and special programs alone cannot eliminate problematic older patrons. Libraries also must provide adequate materials covering topics of interest to older patrons.

Reading is a popular leisure activity for many older adults. User surveys reveal that older patrons enjoy reading magazines and newspapers more than any other type of library material. User surveys also reveal that older patrons prefer reading best-sellers and short stories. They also enjoy materials related to the past such as history and biographies and select reading materials with few sexually explicit references.[16]

Older library patrons have informational needs similar to traditional library patrons. Some older patrons want materials for recreational reading, while others want information to support lifelong learning activities. For the older adult patron, the library is a recreational reading center, consumer information resource, learning facility, information and referral center, social activity center, and a job training facility.

No matter how extensive the collection may be, there will always be someone who says, "Why don't you have the books I want?" From the older adult complaining about pornography to the World War II veteran pointing out historical inaccuracies, every library book or journal may not meet the arbitrary expectations of some patrons.

Library staff also have an obligation to make sure there are materials in all formats. Collection development policies should include purchasing audiovisual materials, such as videos with closed captions, books-on-tape, and large print materials.[17]

One unique phenomenon with large print collections is the tendency for some older patrons to place distinguishing marks in materials that they have read. Problems can result when the library administration requests that the books be cleared of extraneous marks. Allowing the marks to stay in the books is a service to older patrons.

Older patrons are a diverse population group of individuals. They require more, not fewer, choices of materials to satisfy their information needs.[18] Astute library managers realize this and provide older adult patrons a wide assortment of options.

Conclusion

Enlightened library staff recognize that ignoring the special needs of older adults results in frustrated, problematic older adult patrons. Individuals who use a proactive service perspective rarely perceive older adult patrons as problematic. They discredit distinctions between the elderly and other patrons, and anticipate visual, auditory, physical, access, and technology limitations. Effective libraries recognize the diversity among older patrons and provide needed and desired materials. Their staffs adopt an earnest philosophy of patron caring and strive to create a win-win attitude for the library and the older adult patron.

Notes

1. Frank L. Schick and Rene Schick, eds., *Statistical Handbook on Aging America,* 1994 ed. (Phoenix: Oryx Press), 1–2; Jennifer Cheeseman Day, *Current Population Reports: Population Projections of the United States, by Age, Sex, Race and Hispanic Origin: 1993–2050* (Washington, D.C.: U.S. Department of Commerce, Economics and Statistics Administration, Bureau of the Census, 1993), xvii.

2. Celia Hales-Mabry, *The World of the Aging: Information Needs and Choices* (Chicago: American Library Assn., 1993), 9.

3. Roberta Null, "Environmental Design for the Low-Vision Elderly," *Journal of Home Economics* 80, no. 3 (Fall 1988): 29.

4. Hales-Mabry, *The World of the Aging,* 12–14.

5. William L. Needham and Gerald Jahoda, *Improving Library Service to Physically Disabled Persons: A Self-Evaluation Checklist* (Littleton, Colo.: Libraries Unlimited, 1983), 12–13.

6. Hales-Mabry, *The World of the Aging,* 14–15.

7. Irene Burnside, *Working with the Elderly: Group Process and Techniques,* 2nd ed. (Monterey, Calif.: Wadsworth, 1984), 8.

8. Hales-Mabry, *The World of the Aging,* 17.

9. Burnside, *Working with the Elderly,* 10.

10. Elizabeth A. Hudson, *Libraries for a Lifetime* (Oklahoma City: Oklahoma State Department of Libraries, 1989), 47–48.

11. Phileon B. Robinson, "Education for Older Adults," *New Directions for Continuing Education* 20 (Dec. 1983): 67.

12. Ollie Owen, *Computers and the Elderly Program at Syracuse University: A History* (Syracuse, N.Y.: Syracuse University, Kellogg Foundation, 1991), 7.

13. Michael Tingay, *Attitudes and Technologies: Striving to Match New Electronic Information Products and Services to the Needs and Interests of Elderly People* (New York: Aspen Institute for Humanistic Studies, 1988), 3.

14. Gwyneth G. Donchin, *Older Worker Attitudes toward Change and Challenge* (Los Angeles: NATO Symposium on Aging and Technological Advances, 1983), 3.

15. Tingay, *Attitudes and Technologies,* 9.

16. Judith Kamin, "How Older Adults Use Books and the Public Library: A Review of the Literature," Occasional Papers no. 165 (Champaign: Univ. of Illinois Graduate School of Library and Information Science, 1984), 10–11.

17. Hudson, *Libraries for a Lifetime,* 51.

18. Tingay, *Attitudes and Technologies,* 3.

5

Deinstitutionalized and Disabled Patrons: Opportunities and Solutions

Fay Zipkowitz

Of all the populations that public libraries have been responding to in recent years, the deinstitutionalized may be the most perplexing.

The deinstitutionalized may be defined as persons formerly living in institutional settings for physical, mental, learning or emotional disabilities, or persons living in community settings who otherwise likely would be placed in institutions because of these same disabilities. Also, as more disabled children who live at home are mainstreamed into community schools and become part of the community rather than growing up in institutions, they will fall into this category of the new users of public libraries.

In dealing with the deinstitutionalized as with any new or unfamiliar group coming into the library, seeking service and placing demands on staff, the library has had to make adjustments in its response. Determining the needs of these new users, developing appropriate responses to difficult communication transactions, and preparing staff for unexpected behavior are just a few of the issues that library administrators will have to address.

This chapter will focus on some approaches to the issues raised by the advent of deinstitutionalized persons in public libraries. By examining the traditional roles of public libraries and of public librarians in our society, we may be in a better position to respond to new challenges.

The Role of Libraries and Deinstitutionalized Patrons

Public libraries exist as an integral part of a working democracy. The principles underlying public education and public libraries are not simple but they are compelling: people are entitled to use them. Patrons should have equal access to knowledge and the right to participate in the democratic process. They also have the responsibility to participate in that process and to support the institutions that promote universal access to information. (These issues of rights and responsibilities will be of concern throughout this chapter.)

Another important consideration for public institutions such as libraries is the principle of the implied social contract. Individuals make concessions in aspects of their personal freedom for the public good and expect the same from others. There are rules and expectations about public behavior and most people learn them early and well. Most library staff and patrons have been socialized systematically, learning how to behave in public places such as theaters, restaurants, stores, banks, playgrounds, schools, and libraries. We know when to raise our voices and when to modulate them. We know when to control our physical gestures and expressions. We know what reasonable expectations are and which of our desires may be unreasonable. We know what is expected of us and what our responsibilities are. It is this social contract which keeps society going on a daily basis, from the workplace, to obeying traffic laws, to paying taxes, to using libraries.

When this contract is breached, most individuals are shocked and disoriented. When people don't behave in expected ways, others around them don't know how to respond. Our socialization causes us to recoil. The rules do not seem to apply; the norms are not being followed. The ordinary transactions of daily life, including working, become difficult. These temporary disruptions are the cause for much of library workers' anxiety as they try to respond to newer populations, such as deinstitutionalized people, in communities and libraries.

Traditional library patrons have been socialized in the same ways as library staff. For the most part they understand the expected behavior, the way the system works, the role of public institutions. If they object to or question a rule or procedure, library staff can usually explain the workings of the library in ways they can understand and accept even if they do not agree with them or like them. Library workers also feel they have backing and support in the form of the implied social contract. Aberrations in behavior disruptive to the library's purpose, to other patrons and library services should not be tolerated; the ability of library workers to do their jobs needs to be defended.

Who the Deinstitutionalized Are and What They Expect

Massachusetts, where more than one revolution started, was one of the first states to move people out of institutions and into the community and to mainstream the deinstitutionalized into traditional school settings. That adequate preparations were not always in place for these transitions does not negate the worthiness of the intent to move people with disabilities out of state institutions, isolated home settings, special training institutions, and the attics and back rooms of houses. The principle again revolves around rights—rights to adequate living conditions, to educational opportunities, and to responsible participation in society.

Who are these people? First, they are individuals. These are people who, because of one or more disabilities, have been placed in structured, controlled institutional settings, perhaps segmented or partitioned by type of disability such as mental, physical, or emotional. They might have remained in these settings permanently in an earlier part of our history, but due to current practices are not there, or they have been in and out of them. They are also people who have been out of sight at home, limited in mobility and means and therefore, homebound. But above all they are individuals. They are nice or not nice; they are kind or not kind; they are educated or not educated; they are attractive or not pleasant to look at; they are articulate or not. They have needs, desires, emotions, histories, and futures. They may be angry or confrontational based on their past experiences and their difficulties in getting ordinary things done. Each new encounter for them may be a struggle. Each new person they meet is a new challenge—to gain acceptance, credibility, respect, and the appropriate response to their requests. And many deinstitutionalized people have not had the early and continuous socialization that most people have had. Their world view has been circumscribed by their circumstances—where they lived before, where they live now, how they were raised and educated, and how much of the outside world they have been able to cope with. As with our traditional patrons, they need different resources and services at different times in their lives.

These patrons are not really new to us in the library field. Dealing with unusual or unexpected behavior is not a novelty to public library staff. Every community has had a share of people out of the mainstream, the "characters" or the so-called "problem patrons." Libraries have had them almost since libraries began.

What is different now is the number of the individuals and the degree of their problems. There are greater numbers of homeless people, more people with various disabilities not seen in libraries before, people the system has failed, and people who in earlier periods of history would be timid, resigned to their fate, or cowed and grateful for charity. These people are now making demands, asserting their rights and trying to take on the responsibility of full citizenship. Even in library schools we now have people with learning disabilities, disabled veterans, and physically challenged people requiring wheelchairs, signers, note takers, taped lectures, and other adaptive solutions. These people probably would not have been in graduate educational programs twenty or thirty years ago. Some are good students and some are not, but they expect the same opportunities to learn and to succeed as other students have had.

Today, as has been the case historically, librarians do not have enough money to do all the necessary things, let alone all the things we want to do. Public libraries have never been overfunded, but have had to struggle with shifting priorities and diminishing funds. However, libraries may now be in the position of having to reduce services to some of our more traditional patrons—not a pleasant situation.

Another important characteristic of many deinstitutionalized people is that they are a changing and somewhat transient population. Many of them may be in and out of the community, in and out of institutional settings or community residences. They may not have the stability or continuity that library staff are accustomed to from more traditional patrons. This aspect affects the ability of librarians to plan for services and to justify changes in our procedures and collections.

An Opportunity, Not a Burden: Americans with Disabilities Act

Opportunity is the key word when it comes to persons with disabilities: hook that on to rights and responsibilities. The Americans with Disabilities Act (ADA) is designed to enable more people to benefit from what society has to offer, and to contribute to it as well. This is not the place to review the requirements of ADA since there are plenty of guidelines and publications for librarians to study for implementation assistance.

A student of the author of this chapter attended a presentation on ADA at a state library conference. It was entirely legalistic—what is the minimum you absolutely have to do, what can you get away with, what can you fob off, and how to avoid getting sued. The same student later attended a workshop designed to present a view of the ADA as an opportunity:

What can libraries do to expand access, to create alternatives to business as usual?

Whom can libraries enlist in the efforts?

What can library administrators anticipate and plan for instead of waiting for a crisis or a confrontation?

How can library administrators gather evidence for necessary funding?

Instead of viewing the Disabilities Act as one more burden on an already overloaded library and staff, library workers should see it as a way to serve new patrons, to increase usage and gather wider community support. While this message applies to many areas of library services, it is especially useful in helping to cope with deinstitutionalized people in the community by trying to use ADA in a positive way, not a reactive way.

Plan for New Patrons

What can be done to respond to the new demands of deinstitutionalized patrons on our public libraries? Odiorne's Law states that things that do not change remain the same. First, *plan*. Planning services to any group of individuals includes learning who they are, who is already in the community, and who will be out there soon. Do not wait until the state psychiatric hospital closes or the group halfway house shuts its doors. Learn what is going on in the community now, analyze it, and prepare to respond. Use all the available community resources such as city planners, mental health agencies, rehabilitation centers, social service agencies, state service agencies directly involved with services to special populations, schools, colleges, hospitals, newspapers, and neighbors.

Be Prepared

Remember that the deinstitutionalized and disabled, along with their caregivers or support systems, will probably be on the library's doorstep sooner or later. Pretending they won't be will not prevent it from happening. Libraries are still looked upon as stable, safe, serene places, with kindly, patient, benevolent people working in them and using them. Library staff can be prepared for requests for use, for socialization activities, and for jobs. Set the boundaries appropriately. Library staff know that libraries are not safe havens from the world outside, and this needs to be explained clearly and not hysterically or defensively.

Try to determine the expectations of trustees and library staff as well. In planning and discussions include policies, guidelines, parameters, and incentives for service, transactions, behavior, and accommodation, and remember to write down everything. Unwritten rules may be understood by traditional patrons but not by new ones. When difficult encounters do occur, be prepared for them. When an unreasonable demand is made, be ready to demonstrate why it is not reasonable and cannot be met.

Try to get to the community regarding the library's policies before it gets to the library. When a van pulls up to the library at 7:30 P.M. with twelve people in it with perhaps twenty-five different disabilities among them and their escort wants the library to issue them borrowing cards, it is too late to develop a policy. When the city personnel office sends a job applicant with an institutional history, because someone at the office believes that the position available at the library is low stress when it's not, it's too late. At these times library staff are scrambling for answers.

Libraries have to set procedures in advance to accommodate new borrowers who have no traditional home addresses or references. Libraries have to review the available jobs to determine if tasks can be done differently while still getting the job done. If requests for volunteer placements come to the library from caregivers of community agencies, evaluate them carefully. Simple tasks in the library may still require close supervision or take a great deal longer to complete. Some questions to consider, whether the job is volunteer or paid, include:

How crucial is the time factor?

Is there a work area that will accommodate the worker and a caregiver or supervisor?

How shall we assess the adequacy and accuracy of the work?

What are the options to terminate the position if the person does not work out?

Can a set of tasks be organized which have, in advance, an expected end?

Are there physical or site changes that have to be made?

What are the costs?

Will the library and the candidate both benefit from the experience?

One possible scenario is to schedule a visit for a group of persons with disabilities along with caregivers or an individual and caregiver. In this way library administration can prepare the site, staff, and materials for an introduction rather than reacting to an unexpected visit with a disorganized response. If the patrons and their caregivers view the library staff as allies rather than obstacles, a much better climate for communication is in place for everyone.

Recognize Special Needs

Recognize that library orientations for special needs patrons may not be as quick and simple as for other patrons. If a brief flyer with the library rules and hours of service is posted on the wall it may be sufficient for most new library patrons. But patrons with little or no prior library experience may require a slower, more detailed explanation. Remember that socialization and a sense of responsibility may be lacking, and the deinstitutionalized person literally may not know what a library does and what it expects from its patrons. Some libraries have reported that these new patrons behave well on the first visit and then badly on subsequent ones.

For many new patrons, the library visit is the main benefit, not the reading and learning, at least not initially. Prepare to reinforce and repeat messages given to patrons on the first visit. The very permanence and stability of the library in the community can be a useful aspect of the patron's socialization and education.

Anne Turner, in her book, *It Comes with the Territory* (McFarland, 1993), suggests writing clear, concise rules and making sure they are communicated to all patrons. She further states the need for written manuals, guidelines, and posted notices so that everyone, including staff, knows the ground rules. Kitty Smith suggests responses to specific kinds of behavior and argues for changes in our own attitudes, perceptions, and tolerance in *Serving the Difficult Customer* (Neal-Schuman, 1993).

Use the Library

Library staff can use research skills and knowledge of available resources to find out how to best serve deinstitutionalized patrons. It is crucial to review not only library-related literature but also the literature of the various clinical and treatment disciplines. Additionally, it is important not to overlook fiction for educating and sensitizing staff and community. Seek training materials and trainers from the community such as mental health workers, physical therapists, or caregivers. Set up meetings with community groups, the staffs of other public agencies, and other public library staff to discuss expectations and responses.

Librarians know how to find answers: *networking, searching, and finding*. It's what libraries do for patrons and we need to do it for ourselves.

The Vermont Library Association conference of 1993 featured a video, *A Library Survival Guide* (ALA/Library Video Network, 1986), presented by a mental health professional who led a very practical discussion, in which specific responses to unexpected or threatening behavior were exchanged by library staff. Programs at library meetings or conferences have the added advantage of bringing together staff from differently sized libraries in the region or state. Staff are frequently surprised at how much they have in common, regardless of rural, urban, or suburban settings when they compare experiences with non-traditional patrons. It is important to have an experienced discussion leader to avoid focusing on complaints rather than finding practical solutions.

Listen to Patrons

Listening to patrons is important in providing appropriate services. In many situations the patron may be able to articulate his or her requests in ways that may be accommodated by the library. This takes patience and good listening skills, as well as flexibility, but it can result in a positive outcome. One public library was being challenged by a sometimes homeless person who wanted to see the local newspaper as early in the day as possible to seek housing and employment. However, the library's copies of the paper were delivered in midafternoon. But the patron knew, by virtue of being at the library long before the doors opened, that the distributor dropped a bundle of papers early in the morning at the curbside near the library, then later picked up the bundle and began distribution. The patron discussed this with the circulation desk personnel who transmitted this information to the director of the library. The director contacted the distributor and made arrangements for the library's copies of the paper to be dropped in the library mail slot when the bundle was picked up by the delivery person. The library could then put the newspaper out almost as soon as the library opened its doors. The patron was satisfied and what at first seemed like an extreme demand became a workable arrangement. The library staff listened to the patron and took positive action.

Sometimes a special needs patron will come to rely on one sympathetic staff member and be distressed if he or she is not on duty during a particular visit. Again, active listening and reassurance may help the patron feel comfortable with other staff. A three-way interaction involving the patron, the familiar staff member, and a less familiar coworker might also help the situation. Remember that many deinstitutionalized persons are easily frustrated because of their past experiences. Extra patience and further explanation may be needed simply to overcome distrust or disbelief.

Ensure Administrative Support

Administrative support is crucial in dealing with non-traditional patrons or unusual situations. Staff on the front lines may quickly become frustrated, intimidated, and defensive if they feel their fears and concerns are not being heard by the powers that be. Many staff trained in library work are not interested in being trained as social workers. Building security, the arrangement of staff service points and furnishings, and the mechanisms for summoning help in an emergency are administrative responsibilities. Response to such issues by management enables staff to cope with unexpected or unpleasant encounters with confidence and competence.

Several libraries have described *critical incident report* forms that they have developed; any out-of-the-ordinary experience with a patron is briefly documented and can be shared with other staff. Responses to such future incidents can then be suggested in a staff meeting or training session. This form of documentation also helps in negotiating with service agencies and caregivers for better support of library staff and for developing better strategies to handle difficult encounters.

Involve all library staff in training to anticipate and respond appropriately to new demands. Good policies are not segmented. Staff should know how to respond, what and where the back-up is, what fail-safe mechanisms are in place, and what other colleagues are facing. Administrators several levels removed from the front lines need to be buttonholed and made to understand who is walking through the front door and what is occurring. A few paragraphs of suggested guidelines may get the administrator's attention when a lengthy report may not.

Staff must be assured that their safety, dignity, and rights are protected and that they have management and policy support. Moreover, training activities must be ongoing throughout the library. Communication of concerns and critical incidents should be immediate, direct, and go to the administrative level best suited for a response. Staff should not be undercut by "higher ups"; their continued exposure to difficult patrons or situations should be considered when accommodations or relaxation of rules are requested or demanded by patrons or caregivers.

In one case, a branch library staff member tried to enforce a library rule regarding circulation of a reference book. The assistant director in the central library overruled her, and consequently she was subjected to sarcasm and abuse by the patron. From that time on, the patron felt she was entitled to anything she wanted and regularly reminded the staff member that this was the case. The staff member felt angry, humiliated, and betrayed by the administrator. Moreover, the situation continued, leaving the staff member in an untenable position. Administrators should be especially careful about superseding front-line staff decisions; they should consider the possible repercussions and repeated requests which may result from such decisions.

Conclusion

Public library workers have met many challenges in the history of public libraries and now have the opportunity to meet the challenges of serving the deinstitutionalized as well. The deinstitutionalized people should be viewed as *new constituents,* new *potential patrons,* and *supporters of public libraries.* Library workers have to do what they do best: provide public library service to the community. Library staff need support but should neither resent the responsibility nor surrender the rights.

6

Problems with Patrons in the Academic Library

Emerita M. Cuesta

Saturday morning in the library is a quiet time, especially in the summer. The only patrons in the reading room are two students frantically trying to beat the deadline for turning in late papers for the summer term and an elderly gentleman working his way through the last three months of the *New York Times Book Review*. Since reference service is not available until noon, the only staff member in the area is the circulation desk clerk. It is the clerk's first month on the job and the first time she has worked alone.

A young man approaches the desk. He is neat and personable, dressed in clean jeans and a t-shirt with the university seal. In a quiet, courteous manner, he explains that he is looking for a particular book he is sure the library owns, but he cannot locate it in the online catalog.

"Maybe I can do a quick title search for you" the helpful clerk says. "Our online catalog is so new that people are not quite comfortable with it yet. What is the title?"

"The *Necronomicron.*"

The clerk happens to be a fan of gothic horror fiction. She knows the *Necronomicron,* a book mentioned in several of H. P. Lovecraft's tales, exists only in the author's imagination. She informs the patron. He stares at her for a moment, then leans over the counter to whisper confidentially: "I know they tell you to say that, but you can tell me the truth, can't you?"

Since that first Saturday morning I have dealt with many a problem patron, from the compulsive chatterer who assumed that the librarian could spend hours discussing his master's thesis to the woman who carried on a conversation in several different voices while staring at herself in the mirror. I have explained a million times why the library insists on keeping food and drink away from the stacks. I have. . . .

Does this sound familiar?

Anyone who has worked at a public service desk in a college or university library has one or two war stories to tell. Yet, until recently, academic librarians seemed to be much less concerned with problem patrons than our public library colleagues. With the exception of the relatively small group consisting of book thieves, vandals, sex offenders, and the mentally ill, we have tended to look upon patrons with behavior problems as eccentrics (the retired professor who is still writing his magnum opus and, incidentally, driving the reference staff crazy with his demands) or merely annoyances (the graduate student who insists on further borrowing privileges even though he has five hundred dollars in fines and bills). A quick survey of *Library Literature* for the past five years shows that academic librarians are mostly concerned with protecting their collections against theft and vandalism, with computer/software security running a close second.[1] Whether this concentration on property crimes occurred because the intellectual and monetary investment represented by books, journals, and databases focuses attention on those particular problems, or simply because it is falsely believed that the academic environment is inherently safe, academic librarians have not addressed the issue of the problem patron in any significant fashion.[2]

The current atmosphere of increased awareness and concern over problem patrons is clearly part of a larger societal concern with security and crime prevention. It is undeniable that academic libraries, especially those in urban environments, are experiencing the same kind of social and economic stresses that affect all of our social institutions. As recent news stories have amply demonstrated, a library can no longer be considered a safe haven.

The Academic Library Environment

The perception of academic libraries as ivory towers, dedicated to the pleasures of education and research and insulated from the problems of the "real world," does not hold up well under scrutiny. State-financed colleges and universities are often obliged to provide services to the general public. Many private institutions, either from custom or public pressure, also offer some form of access. Even libraries that are officially closed to the public may have consortia or some other kind of access-sharing arrangements with local or regional institutions or may be federal or state document depositories.

Most importantly, in the last twenty years the academic library's primary clientele has expanded considerably, as colleges and universities offer services to nontraditional patrons. Most academic institutions now have at least one of the following:

programs for retirees;

advanced placement classes for high school students;

certification programs for professionals, paraprofessionals, and technical workers;

job retraining for the recently unemployed or those reentering the workforce;

"enrichment" courses for people developing a hobby or simply wishing to sample the academic life.

This influx of external and nontraditional users has coincided with a long period of stagnant or declining budgets and rising costs. Some libraries have resorted to charging fees to external users, but typically these are cost recovery measures since the library makes little, if any, profit. Overall, academic libraries are struggling to maintain traditional levels of service with less money and staff.

Current financial constraints have also affected staffing patterns in many libraries. In the best of all possible worlds, public service desks would always be staffed by experienced librarians and paraprofessionals. This is not always the case. Academic libraries are usually open until late at night six or seven days a week. Administrators often must rely on adjuncts, part-time workers, and student assistants. The inevitable turnover in this group means that less experienced staff will be more likely to be on duty in the evenings and weekends. With the full-time staff gone, the authority of these people can be compromised. For example, a student assistant may have trouble with a disruptive patron who is a fraternity brother, or, worse yet, one of his or her professors.

Problem Patrons in the Academic Environment

Brashear and his colleagues identified three types of problem patrons in their study of incidence of problem behavior in Illinois public and academic libraries.[3]

Type 1 (Relatively harmless nuisances): persons who do not pose an overt threat or cause disruption, but who generally may be regarded by the staff or other patrons as offensive, such as quiet drunks, persons who sit and stare for hours, or persons who are offensively dirty and foul-smelling.

Type 2 (Disruptive or threatening): those who disrupt other patrons or staff members, or who pose a threat without actually attempting to commit an act of violence, such as exhibitionists, loud drunks, uncontrollably irate patrons, or people who walk around glaring and muttering at other library users.

Type 3 (Violent): persons who commit or attempt to commit an act of violence against a staff member or another patron, such as assault, rape, or child molestation.

There is no doubt that such frightening social trends as homelessness, drug use, and violent crime in the workplace have not spared libraries from their effects. This impact is reflected in the library literature. Martin Sable tabulated articles published between 1876 and 1985 on the subjects of problem patrons, security, and library use regulations and resulting patron relationships. This tabulation shows that after 1970, there is a precipitous increase in the number of articles published on these subjects. The decade of 1970–1979 shows an increase of 717 percent over the previous decade, and the five years from 1980 through the first quarter of 1985 show an increase of 128 percent over 1970–1979.[4] There also seems to be an increase in the *severity* of these incidents, as demonstrated by recent reports of armed assault, hostage-taking, rape, and murder.

However, incidents of illegal or violent behavior represent a small percentage of the problems a public service staffer will encounter. Anecdotal evidence suggests that by far the most common problem is the irate patron. Typically, this person wishes to challenge the library's policies and will not take no for an answer. In some extreme cases irate patrons may become abusive and threatening, but generally they just want to "get it off their chest."

A different kind of problem is posed by the external or nontraditional user. Library staff in academic libraries offering even minimal services to the general public must be ready to assist patrons with a variety of problems not previously encountered on a university campus. If the library is located in an urban area suffering an economic downturn, it may be experiencing a sharp increase in business and job-related reference questions. If the local school budget is decreasing, it may be serving as the primary resource for high school students completing assignments. If the public library is closing branches, weekend staff may be dealing with an influx of elderly patrons.

These patrons can place a strain on the library's services. According to one source, they are "generally more diverse than typical institutional users . . . They may request different types of information and unusual services that are outside of those most frequently used by the academic library's primary clientele."[5] Such patrons often do not have the skills necessary to negotiate the information maze and can be quite vocal about their frustrations. Many, especially elderly patrons, are intimidated by technology and require extensive coaching; on the other hand, the more technically sophisticated are infuriated by restrictions on use.

It is not the author's intention to imply that we should view all external or nontraditional library users as potential problems. In fact, as previously mentioned, a public service staffer is more likely to have a confrontation with a student than with a visitor. However, their needs and expectations add yet another layer of complexity to the duties of the staffer at a time when we are beginning to feel overwhelmed.

There is another type of patron that seems to be peculiar, to a great extent, to the academic environment, *Type 4 (The dignitary nuisance)*. A dignitary nuisance can best be defined as a person in a position of authority or influence within the academic community who is certain that library rules apply to everyone but him- or herself.

Coping with Problem Patrons in the Academic Environment

Dealing with overtly disruptive, illegal, or violent behavior is often a matter of applying existing policies. An Association of Research Libraries (ARL) Office of Management Services survey of building security and personal safety in research libraries found that "it is more common for libraries to have policies governing the more severe forms of problem behavior that threaten life or property, than the milder forms which affect the rights of individuals to work undisturbed in libraries."[6] However, it is the nuisances (types 1 and 4) which will often present the greatest dilemma to the public service staffer. What do you do about the guy working quietly at a table in the reference area whose body odor is driving people out of the room? Or the influential tenured professor that loudly and belligerently proclaims his right to search the patron records to discover who has checked out the only copy of *Dubliners* owned by the library?

The etiquette of our profession requires us "to respond to all patrons in a courteous and informative manner . . . to demonstrate kindness, patience, caring, and respect . . . to uphold the rules without being tyrannical . . . to answer questions speedily, efficiently, and comprehensively."[7] Unfortunately, although long on philosophy, this code is woefully short on practical advice. In most instances it is the judgment and common sense of the staffer that will determine the outcome of any patron interaction. Each incident will be unique, requiring a specific response.

The library administration can support the public service staff in two ways: (1) develop well-defined guidelines that address common types of disruptive behavior; and (2) set up an in-service training program focused on diagnosis and prevention.

Guidelines

A comprehensive security policy should include at least the following:[8]

1. A conduct policy that spells out what is considered unacceptable behavior in the library
2. General tips for the staffer on dealing with a disturbed or angry patron
3. Descriptions of types of unacceptable behavior (verbal abuse, bizarre but non-threatening acts, suspected theft, etc.), together with procedures for dealing with each one
4. Names and home telephone numbers of supervisory personnel to be called in emergencies
5. The number of the campus safety office or local police department
6. Samples of all reports that must be completed for each type of incident, whether internal (to the attention of the staffer's immediate supervisor) or external (campus safety or police documentation).

The security policy should be part of the library's policies and procedures manual. The importance of a manual that standardizes routine procedures cannot be overemphasized. A good manual establishes precedent, communicates the rationale for each procedure, and defines individual responsibility at each step in the chain of command. It can be very effective in defusing public confrontation. For example, in the case of the belligerent professor, the staffer can show him the section dealing with confidentiality of patron records and refer him to the appropriate department head for further consultation.

For a manual to be effective, it must make a clear distinction between policies and procedures. Policies provide "guidelines employees can follow consistently without referring to higher level of authority. Accordingly . . . (they) provide a framework for the delegation of decision-making, eliminate misunderstandings, and reduce uncertainties."[9] It is the responsibility of the library administration to outline policy in such a manner that it is neither "so broad as to be meaningless or inhibit understanding nor so narrow as to stifle initiative."[10] Procedures, on the other hand, "tells employees how to perform tasks or groups of tasks . . . (they) describe what should take place; they are the standard against which practices are measured."[11] Staff at every level should have input in designing the procedures. This is especially important when dealing with security issues, since public services staffers will have experience in dealing with problems and will have valuable advice to pass on. When drafting procedures, the administration primarily should be concerned that the procedures meet the university's legal standards.

Once the manual is compiled, each staff member should receive a copy. Familiarity with operational rules should be required of all library staff. Library administration should also make every effort to familiarize the academic community with the library policies and procedures. Many a difficult encounter can be avoided if students, faculty, administrators, and alumni are informed of library policies.

All the familiarity in the world, however, will not reassure a staffer whose decisions are second-guessed by management. Although there is no doubt that sometimes administrators will have to reassess a staffer's decision in view of diplomacy, faculty politics, or other external factors, it is very important that those on the front lines feel that the library administration will support them.

Training

Policy and procedures manuals alone will not be sufficient to help a staff member spot problems before they escalate. As Shuman states, "since few library employees have training in psychology, and since even Viennese psychiatrists cannot predict anyone's behavior with confidence, there are too many random variables at play to derive certain rules or laws of optimal reaction, on the part of the library staff."[12] Competence in predicting the "trouble quotient" of any situation comes to most of us through years of experience, and even the most experienced among us can call it wrong.

To help staff hone these skills, in-house seminars and workshops focusing on diagnosis and prevention of problem behavior should be an integral part of any library's staff development program. Good training not only helps staffers cope with a patron's behavior, but teaches them to control their own attitudes and maintain a professional, detached manner. Role-playing, case studies, assertiveness techniques, and customer-care training are among the methods recommended.[13]

Some administrators have expressed fear that staffers trained in these techniques may be too willing to enter into a confrontation with a patron. Brashear notes that a common refrain from respondents was that "the library administration, secure in the rear area, did not wish to admit to and face the problem."[14] In the academic setting, these fears seem to spring mostly from the need to maintain good relations with other units within the academic community, as well as with the community at large. This unrealistic attitude is crumbling under the weight of current library crime statistics. Faced with a rise in disruptive, threatening, and even violent behavior, administrators have begun to address the question of the safety and well-being of employees and patrons. They have discovered that a well-prepared staff is our first and best tool in the battle to maintain a secure environment.

Conclusions

The clerk takes stock of the situation. Her only student assistant is somewhere in the stacks, retrieving some books to be placed on reserve. The closest telephone is behind her on her desk; there are no emergency buttons near. Quickly, she leans over the counter and whispers:

"Look, all I can say is that we don't have a copy."

The young man smiles knowingly. "Not here. But other places?"

The clerk shrugs. The young man gives her a conspiratorial nod and leaves the library, whistling.

Did I do the right thing? To this day I am not certain. I do know that something about that mild-mannered young man set off every one of my internal alarms. There was nothing in the library's security procedures to cover this kind of incident; I made my decision based on a hunch and my knowledge of Lovecraft's works. It worked, but it might just as well have landed me in a confrontation with a mentally unstable man.

I should point out that in the twelve years I have worked in libraries, I can only recall two incidents of this kind (the lady who talked to herself in the mirror is the other). The overwhelming majority of my confrontations with patrons have been over library policies and procedures.

A good policy and procedures manual and some interpersonal skills training can help even the neophyte staffer cope in an awkward situation such as the one described above. Each library will ultimately decide which security measures are appropriate to their environment and financial resources. It is important to realize, however, that security is an ongoing process requiring regular fine-tuning in order to be successful. Policies and procedures should be reviewed at regular intervals to weed out inaccuracies and contradictions. After an incident, the staffer involved should be asked to point out any deficiencies in the security policy. There also should be a regular program of workshops or seminars that address new problems. With this foundation, staffers will be better equipped to handle a problem patron calmly and efficiently.

NOTES

1. The following topics were examined: crime in the library, computer security, discipline in the library, safety measures, access to libraries, and theft and losses of books, periodicals, etc.

2. Elizabeth Ader and Julie Pinnell, "Security and Safety of People in Urban Academic Libraries," in *Academic Libraries in Urban and Metropolitan Areas: A Management Handbook,* ed. Gerard McCabe (Westport, Conn.: Greenwood, 1991), 173–85.

3. J. Kirk Brashear, James J. Maloney, and Judellen Thorton-Darringe, "Problem Patrons: The Other Kind of Library Security," *Illinois Libraries* 63 (April 1981), 344.

4. Martin H. Sable, "Problem Patrons in Public and University Libraries," *Encyclopedia of Library and Information Science* 43 (New York: Marcel Dekker, 1988), 174–75.

5. Ralph E. Russell, Carolyn L. Robison, James E. Prather, et al., "External User Access to Academic Libraries in Urban/Metropolitan Areas," in *Academic Libraries in Urban and Metropolitan Areas: A Management Handbook,* ed. Gerard McCabe (Westport, Conn.: Greenwood, 1991), 27.

6. Association of Research Libraries, Office of Management Services, *Building Security and Personal Safety,* SPEC Kit no. 150 (Washington, D.C.: ARL, 1989).

7. Janette S. Caputo, *Stress and Burnout in Libraries* (Phoenix: Oryx, 1991), 13.

8. For examples of security policies, see Association of Research Libraries, SPEC Kit no. 150: *Building Security and Personal Safety.*

9. Stuart Bloom, "Policies and Procedures That Communicate," *Personnel Journal* (Sept. 1983), 712.

10. Ibid., 714.

11. Ibid., 712.

12. Bruce A. Shuman, "Problem Patrons in Libraries—A Review Article," *Library & Archival Security* 9, no. 2 (1989): 3–19.

13. Colin Braddock, "Centering Crime: A Model Training Program for Managers," in *Security and Crime Prevention in Libraries* (Aldershot, Eng., and Brookfield, Vt.: Ashgate, 1992), and Elena Cevallos, and Charles Kratz, "Training for Public Services," *Journal of Library Administration* 12, no. 2 (1990), 27–45.

14. Brashear, "Problem Patrons," 351.

II

What Are the Issues?

7

Crime in Academic Libraries

Mary M. Harrison, Alison Armstrong, and David Hollenbeck

How extensive is crime in academic libraries? Are staff, patrons, and collections safe? What "incidents" has the library experienced within the past two years: arson, theft, indecent exposure, to name a few?

Crime in general is on the rise and there is no reason to believe that academic libraries are bucking the national trend.[1] Although there are no current statistics on the amount and types of crime in academic libraries, a scan of recent news articles clearly indicates a disturbing pattern.

The Scope of the Problem

The exact amount of destruction to academic library collections is hard to pinpoint, but in one of the few surveys done on theft and mutilation of library materials, Terri Pedersen asserts that "the problem of periodical and book theft and mutilation is laying waste to vital and expensive library collections throughout the country."[2] Many academic libraries such as Stanford, William and Mary, Penn State, Washington State University, Harvard, and Notre Dame have been in the news due to major losses of books from their collections.[3]

Another area of concern infrequently reported is the extent that library materials are checked out and simply not returned. One expensive area of theft is electronic equipment: computers, audiovisual equipment, and phones. The cost to each library is unknown, but all libraries have similar considerations regarding crime and security. While many of the costs of theft to libraries are easily identifiable, some are "hidden." For example:

1. Initial outlay for security systems and the costs of staffing and maintaining those systems
2. Extra staffing and effort for periodicals collections, particularly the care and maintenance of current reading rooms
3. Attention to rare books and special collections
4. Stacks maintenance and security patrols
5. The inconvenience and cost of replacement materials
6. The loss of irreplaceable items.

Protection of material is not the only concern of academic libraries. Protecting patrons and staff has been documented recently enough to indicate that violent crime, though unusual, is on the rise in many libraries. California, Arizona, and Utah have had violent crimes in libraries recently.[4] Crimes against people may also include disruptive and nuisance behavior. This type of crime is harder to document, although many librarians have been faced with behavior they would describe as disruptive. Over the past decade, articles and books on this subject have appeared with increasing frequency.[5] Academic libraries are now facing crimes which, in the past, occurred more often in public libraries, with urban libraries bearing the brunt of the crimes.

Whether society has become more violent remains for sociologists and criminologists to determine. The truth is that academic libraries must now provide security not only for their collections but also for their staff and patrons. A recent issue of *School Library Journal* presented an editorial of benefit to all libraries regarding the security issue.[6]

After a string of murders in libraries throughout the United States, library staff who are faced with a disgruntled patron who cannot find a book, who may be extremely angry about a large fine, or who is denied use of a collection, must now determine if the patron is simply angry and letting off steam, or if the patron is unbalanced and may actually harm someone.

An unnecessary call from staff to campus security sometimes risks ridicule from other staff or the officers. However, to let the patron rant and rave may indicate to others that you are not in charge and are letting the patron berate you or other staff.

Threats against staff and others may be muttered by a patron under his or her breath, and the staff member may not be sure just what was mumbled. This happened at one author's library, and the staff member called security after hearing a patron mention killing everyone. After officers interviewed the patron, who assured the officers that he had said no such thing, the campus police reassured the staff that they should always call and let the officers talk to the person. The staff was advised not to confront the patron and that security staff were better trained in interviewing techniques. Other types of threatening behaviors are stalking (and many states have or are in the process of enacting anti-stalking laws), assaults, abusive behavior, language, and intimidation.[7]

Arson is another very dangerous crime and endangers not only the library's collections but also its staff and patrons as well. Obscene phone calls and indecent exposure are nuisances but still very unpleasant for staff and patrons.

The rest of this chapter is divided into two sections. The first concerns nuisance patrons and the second deals with more serious problem patrons. The examples are from the actual experiences of librarians at one particular urban academic library, but they can apply to most academic libraries. The authors reviewed the crime reports from the campus police from a three-and-one-half year period at the urban library.[8] Over one-half of the reported crimes were theft of personal property. The remaining crimes ranged from obscene behavior to arson.

Nuisance Patrons

A nuisance patron is defined as "one that is annoying, unpleasant, or obnoxious." Nuisance patrons are the type most librarians are likely to deal with but they are not life-threatening. These can be students listening to music through earphones that can be heard ten feet away. When asked to lower the volume, most patrons will do so and quickly apologize for annoying others. There is always one who complains and refuses to see that someone else may be bothered. This type of problem can be covered with a simple library policy stating no radios, CDs, or tapes may be used in the library. The same policy may be applied to cellular phones. It is very annoying for studying patrons to be subjected to the constant ringing of several phones in a quiet reference room. Some universities have banned phones and beepers in classrooms and the library.[9]

Another nuisance patron is one who tries intimidation to get attention. This includes patrons with loud voices, the "squeaky wheel types." Many try to get more privileges by berating staff.

In the same vein is patron use of abusive or obscene language. While this type of language has become commonplace in casual conversation, it is still offensive to many staff who work public service desks. This conduct is now categorized as harassment, and many states have laws protecting employees from this abusive behavior. Nevada has such a law and many libraries are now posting copies of this law in prominent places, such as at all public service desks.[10] In the academic setting, such offensive behavior is often reported to the student affairs office where the offending party is called in and counseled regarding proper behavior before formal charges are made. This action usually remedies the situation. The student conduct code usually addresses these predicaments. The problem becomes more involved when the abusive patron is a public patron who is not subject to the student conduct code. Sometimes campus police will interview the patron and, if deemed a nuisance, he or she will be "trespassed," meaning the person cannot return to campus for a set period of time. If the patron returns, he or she can be arrested and turned over to the city police.

When a staff member is faced with an abusive or disruptive patron, the person has several options. One is to quietly answer the patron, thereby helping the patron to lower his or her voice. If that does not work, the person can be referred to a supervisor. Often, by the time the patron gets to the proper office, he has cooled off and much of the anger has been defused. If this does not work and the staff person feels threatened, the staff member can excuse himself or herself and go to another office and call a supervisor or campus security.

In urban academic libraries, the homeless have become a problem. Street people often come in and spend the day roaming the library. Some even stash their belongings, especially if the library offers lockers for patrons to store materials while using the library. Some may even attempt to spend the night, evading the staff at closing time, and hiding themselves in bathrooms, study carrels, storage rooms, and so forth. It is incumbent upon staff to be very diligent in checking the building before closing time. Staff are often reluctant to confront persons found hiding, so some libraries now use student security, trained by campus police, to help secure libraries. Others have the campus police check the library building carefully after the staff leaves.

Another disruptive but usually non-violent personality type is the patron who exposes himself to others. While this is unpleasant to most people, this type of person rarely goes any further. Persons witnessing this type of behavior are usually nonplussed and the perpetrator often escapes before the incident is reported. Library staff often get a general description of the exposer and try to watch for him. These individuals are difficult to catch as they expose themselves in isolated stacks or other out-of-the-way places. They then leave the library before security can arrive.

Threatening Patrons

Patrons who are mentally unbalanced are harder to contend with, as they often appear rational until provoked by some perceived slight. Paranoids and schizophrenics are difficult to deal with as they can become violent at any point. Campus police usually advise library staff to treat all threats as real and to report them as soon as can be done safely. Some libraries devise "code" words to let others know a staff member feels threatened. The police are then notified by a staff member who is away from the situation. Another way to notify campus security is to install "panic buttons" at service desks. These are tied directly into the campus security headquarters. Security responds by sending someone to the area and calling the desk to verify trouble. Again, a code word will let the caller know there is a problem and that the person at the desk is unable to respond.

Library staff are usually not trained to handle unbalanced persons who might become aggressive or violent. Staff should be aware that this type of behavior can occur and should not take patrons of this sort into a private office or into an isolated area. It is also important to have witnesses or help should the situation escalate before the proper authorities arrive.

Arson is also a threatening situation. Although it may be hard to catch an arsonist, any library who has a firebug must vigorously attack this problem. Once it is known that a library is threatened by arson, several avenues can be taken. One is to organize staff to patrol the building at random times. This was done at one author's library. Another is to make every worker aware of the problem so they can watch for suspicious behavior. This may take valuable time from work but it must be done, especially if the library does not have the funds to hire extra security for patrol. Everyone from the dean to student shelvers can help prevent fires in a building. A third way is to hire security for patrolling the library. This is expensive but a highly effective choice.

Guidelines and Preventative Measures

Academic libraries, especially those in urban areas, should provide policies and procedures for problem patrons. While it is not necessary to describe each possible situation, it is important to have a written procedure so all staff will know who to call and what to do and not do in a given situation.

Training sessions should also be held to make staff aware of the variety of problems they may face. Role playing often helps staff deal with problems. A good training program will address situations and provide possible solutions. Campus police departments are usually willing to conduct training sessions in the library for staff and student workers.

Also, as soon as a problem is identified, all staff should be notified in order to be aware of a potential situation they may face. All service desk personnel should be notified as soon as possible of existing situations as well as descriptions of the persons involved. Another way to eliminate possible situations is to have good, bright lighting in all areas of a library. The elimination of dark corners is a deterrent to some types of behavior. Isolated rooms should be eliminated if possible or patrolled on an irregular basis.

When a library has to hire guards or have campus security safeguard the library, these patrols should be highly visible. They should also be irregular so that problem patrons will not be able to time their routes. Highly visible signs should be posted throughout the library telling users that security is available. Signs are often posted to make users aware of thieves but rarely does one see signs promoting security checks. If the library cannot afford outside security, often library staff make checks throughout the building to help users feel more safe. If staff members have to secure the building at closing time, it is better to do so in pairs.

For libraries that can afford to do so, surveillance cameras placed throughout the library often deter crime and make it easier to identify perpetrators. The cost is not only for the equipment but also for someone to monitor the cameras the entire time the library is open.

The best way to prevent crime is to make staff and users aware of the types and consequences of crime. Student government associations might offer safety awareness programs as part of the orientation of new students. Also campus security can conduct programs for dormitory dwellers as well as for the library. An alert clientele is a first line of defense against crime.

The most important way to deter crime is to prosecute those who are caught committing crimes. The business world has demonstrated this with its prosecution of shoplifters. Perhaps we as librarians should follow suit.

Issues

One of the biggest issues is the balance between security and freedom. Libraries that are armed fortresses are hardly conducive to intellectual freedom and the pursuits of higher learning. Another issue concerns individual rights and the ability to protect the collection. Can libraries fix blame? Can we really ascertain who has damaged what material? Cost of staff time and materials is another issue. And finally, not infrequently, in the cases of rare books or materials from special collections, the thieves are library staff.

Solutions

Written and practiced library procedures and policies should clearly state the library's stance on theft and mutilation of materials. If patrons believe they will be caught for theft they are less likely to steal. If patrons have easy access to photocopying or if there is free photocopying, they will be less likely to damage material, particularly periodical and reference material.

Publicity campaigns which post signs with messages indicating fines and penalty for theft, and time and cost of replacement of materials, are usually effective. Allowing reference materials and periodicals to circulate may be a solution for some libraries.

The solution to theft of rare books or materials from special collections poses a different sort of problem. These areas need to be guarded as valuable art collections are guarded. Surveillance mirrors and cameras are also deterrents to theft. Again, the posting of penalties often deters users from theft. Public awareness programs highlighting the types of crimes and cautioning users to watch their own items can deter crime. Campus police sometimes offer "Gotcha" cards, to be placed on users' backpacks, purses, and so forth, when a staff member finds them unattended.

Destruction of library property, such as destroying cards from the card catalog, altering hard drives on computers, infecting software with viruses, and defacing books and materials are harder to deter. These usually occur when no one is around. Library staff and students must be vigilant against these crimes as they can totally destroy a database, which can be extremely expensive to replace.

Libraries cannot afford to ignore safety and security issues. Yet implementing security procedures and systems demands time and money on the part of already over-burdened and under-funded institutions. Still, in terms of patron and collection safety, an ounce of prevention is worth a pound of cure.

Notes

1. Douglas Lederman, "Colleges Report Rise in Violent Crime," *Chronicle of Higher Education,* Feb. 3, 1995, p.31.

2. Terri L. Pedersen, "Theft and Mutilation of Library Materials," *College & Research Libraries* 51, no. 2 (March 1990): 120.

3. Sheila O'Keefe, "Libraries Face Many Exposures, Costly Losses," *National Underwriter Casualty Risk Benefits Management* (June 1, 1993): 12.

4. Evan St. Lifer, "How Safe Are Our Libraries?" *Library Journal* 119 (Aug. 1994): 35.

5. Michael Chaney and Alan F. MacDougal, eds., *Security and Crime Prevention in Libraries* (Aldershot, Eng., and Brookfield, Vt.: Ashgate, 1992).

6. Lillian Gerhardt, "Safe at Work?: Library Security Strategies for Staff Protection," *School Library Journal* 39, no. 2 (Feb. 1993): 4.

7. *Nevada Revised Statutes* 199.30.

8. University of Nevada Las Vegas Campus Police, *Statistics Report,* June 1994.

9. University of Nevada Las Vegas, *Student Conduct Handbook,* 1994.

10. *Policy and Procedure Manual,* University of Nevada Las Vegas Library, 1993.

BIBLIOGRAPHY

Raeder, Aggi. "Protecting Your Most Important CD-ROM Assets: AUTOMENU to the Rescue." *Online* 14, no. 6 (Nov. 1990): 116.

Sherbine, Karen. "Closing the Book on Library Losses." *Best's Review (Property/Casualty Insurance Edition)* 93, no. 4 (Aug. 1992): 64.

8
Legal Issues regarding Library Patrons

Katherine Malmquist

Libraries seldom make news headlines in regard to legal cases involving patrons. When there is local or even national attention for libraries it is usually about patron access to information. Three areas of concern are reviewed in this chapter: patron access to the library, patron requests for copyrighted material (access to specific information), and patron requests for assistance at the reference desk (access to assistance for information). To understand the rights and responsibilities of libraries and patrons one must first understand the law as it applies to various legal matters.

Access to the Library

Access policies vary depending on the types of libraries. A discussion of these follow.

Public Libraries

Access to the public library by anyone is a limited right, according to the courts. There can be access policies for the public but these limitations must be carefully worded and limited in scope. In many towns, both large and small, the public library is a symbol of access to information for recreational and educational purposes. When entering a library most patrons expect the peace and quiet of a studious place. But with the openness of the library comes the variety of patron personalities that can lead to problems for both the library and other patrons.

In *Kreimer v. Bureau of Police for the Town of Morristown, et al.,* 958 F.2d 1242 (3rd Cir. 1992), Richard Kreimer, a homeless man, challenged the notion that a library, in this case the Joint Free Public Library of Morristown and Morris Township, could deny his access to the building and in doing so, to the information it holds. Mr. Kreimer claimed he came to the library to quietly read or to contemplate, but the library stated his behavior was offensive and disruptive to other patrons. This disruptive behavior included staring at and following patrons, talking loudly, and emitting an offensive odor.

The library board, worried about ensuring all patrons the peaceful use of the library, had written a set of library rules. The rules included prohibiting certain patron behavior and allowing for the expulsion of anyone who violated the rules. While these rules were in effect Mr. Kreimer was expelled twice for breaking the rules.

Mr. Kreimer sued the library, as well as other parties, for access to the library. The District Court in New Jersey ruled in Mr. Kreimer's favor, stating that the three applicable rules of the library policy were partially unconstitutional since they violated the freedom of speech, due process, and equal protection rights of the homeless (*Kreimer v. Bureau of Police for the Town of Morristown, et al.,* 765 F.Supp. 181 [1991]). The decision was appealed to the Court of Appeals which stated that the right to receive information under the First Amendment's protection of freedom of speech is not an unfettered right and may give way to significant countervailing interests. It also pointed out that the public library is a limited or designated public forum where constitutional protection is afforded only to activities consistent with the nature of a library. As such, the appeals court, using a "reasonable" standard, examined the three library rules that were used against Mr. Kreimer. Rule 1 provided that "patrons shall be engaged in activities associated with the use of a public library while in the building. Patrons not engaged in reading, studying, or using library materials shall be required to leave the building." The court held that this rule was reasonable and valid as it only prohibited activities beyond the purpose of a library. The rule also listed the criteria for library officials to follow, and, as such, it could not be struck down on account of vagueness or the possibility of unfair or discriminatory practices.

Rule 5 stated that "patrons shall respect the rights of other patrons and shall not harass or annoy others through noisy or boisterous activities, by staring at another person with the intent to annoy that person, by following another person about the building with the intent to annoy that person, by playing audio equipment so that others can hear it, by singing or talking loudly to others or in monologues, or by behaving in a manner which reasonably can be expected to disturb other patrons." The court pointed out that this rule is reasonable and valid as it only prohibits behavior that tends to be disruptive in a library setting. The rule also listed specific behavior and so could not be struck down on the basis of vagueness.

Lastly, the court examined Rule 9 which stated "patrons whose bodily hygiene is offensive so as to constitute a nuisance to other persons shall be required to leave the building." The court held that this rule was reasonable and valid, as it only prohibited behavior that was disruptive, but did not bar a patron from permanently entering the library, and had a level that the behavior must reach before expulsion (nuisance). The court went on to state that while the library's standard of "nuisance" was broad, it was not necessarily vague and unconstitutional. It would be impossible to list all the various factual predicates of a nuisance, and the court pointed out that the term "nuisance" allowed the library to use an objective reasonableness test. The right to receive information can be limited with a narrowly tailored restriction that does not improperly prohibit patrons from exercising their constitutional rights.

A later case, *Brinkmeier v. City of Freeport,* 1993 WL 248201 (N.D.Ill.), July 2, 1993, showed what type of rules would not be allowed by a court. Mr. Brinkmeier alleged that his First Amendment rights were violated when he was prohibited from using the Freeport Public Library. In this case, it was alleged that Mr. Brinkmeier, outside the library, had harassed a library employee who was leaving work. The harassment entailed a note to the employee that contained sexually offensive material. When Mr. Brinkmeier showed up in the library the next day, the police were called and he left voluntarily when advised that the library wanted him to leave. His return to the library a few days later caused the director to sign a trespass notice prohibiting Mr. Brinkmeier from entering the library. During these expulsions the library had an unwritten policy that precluded entry into the library to any patron who "harasses or intimidates other library patrons or employees."

In the *Brinkmeier* case, the court followed the *Kreimer* decision by reiterating that a public library is not a traditional public forum but a designated public forum, and therefore library users may not engage in certain expressive conduct ordinarily associated with traditional public forums. Being a designated public forum allowed for only certain types of expressive activities, such as the communication of the written word, and need not be open to all First Amendment activities. The court then reviewed the unwritten policy and stated that it was overly broad and lacked reasonable limitations of conduct. While an unwritten rule is not in itself unconstitutional, it does lend itself to a myriad of problems, including proof of existence. The court held that the terms "harassing" and "intimidating" were not defined in terms that involved the use of a library.

The court went on to state that the policy also failed to place a geographical limitation on where the harassment or intimidation was not to occur. For example the phrase did not delineate between behavior occurring miles from the library and in the library. In this specific case, the offensive letter was handed to the library employee outside of the library as she left work. There were no reasonable guidelines on such proscribed behavior. The court further stated that there was not a time limitation on the banishment from the library in the policy. Under the unwritten policy, a patron might be banned forever from the library for a single minor instance of misbehavior.

The last point the court made was that there was not any type of procedural safeguard whereby a patron might challenge the denial of access to the library. While there need not be a formal procedure in place, the court felt that a lack of *any* procedure would allow a conclusion that the policy is less than reasonable.

Given these two court decisions, *Kreimer* and *Brinkmeier*, libraries that want to protect themselves from adverse decisions of courts should do the following:

1. Develop written policies. These written rules should be in place before any action is taken, and they should be open for public review. Policies that only a few select patrons know about and policies that suddenly appear out of nowhere lend themselves to suspicion by courts. Note how the court in *Brinkmeier* questioned the unwritten library rules that were in place.
2. Rules should be as specific as possible and limited to patron conduct *in* the library. They should also be based on the purposes of the library. Policies should list specific conduct that would be disruptive to or interfere with the use of the library by other patrons. Examine the wording of the phrases in the *Kreimer* library policies. Then note how the library policy in *Brinkmeier* was considered too broad and undefined.
3. Have written procedures for patrons who want to appeal an expulsion. They do not have to be formal procedures, but they should allow a patron who questions the denial of access to the library an opportunity to prove extenuating circumstances or request a limitation of the library's actions.

Academic and Other Types of Libraries

Access to other types of libraries may be less of a right than for public libraries. Academic libraries are sometimes limited in their access.

As an example, in *Commonwealth v. Downing*, 470 A.2d 526 (Pa.Super. 1983) the access involved the use of Temple University's Law School Library during examinations when limited-use restrictions had been imposed. During exams, special permission was needed for access to the library by non-university patrons. Mr. Downing, who was not affiliated with the university, periodically used the law library with a general pass from the law school. During one of the limited-use restrictions Mr. Downing was refused admittance. A memo was prepared that day and sent to the university security office stating that the defendant was not to be admitted. However, the defendant again returned and was escorted off university premises. The defendant immediately returned to the law library, where he was arrested at the check-out desk. The defendant was convicted of defiant trespass in municipal court and appealed to the superior court.

In reversing the conviction, the superior court held that the library was open to the public under Pennsylvania statute and that the defendant complied with all lawful conditions under the statute. On appeal, the Supreme Court of Pennsylvania reversed and remanded the case (*Commonwealth v. Downing*, 511 A.2d 792 [Pa. 1986]), holding that the library did not need to be open to the public because the law library was private property. It is interesting to note that even though Temple University is a federal depository library, the limited restrictions were still valid because the government documents would have been available to Mr. Downing at another time or place.

Private academic libraries can limit access to their collection, but public academic libraries must consider the laws of their state and the policies of the institution. Very few cases regarding academic library access have ever made it to a court of law. This does not mean that there will not be future cases, so following the stated principles regarding public library access might afford some protection.

If limitations are to be enforced, they should be limited in time and place. Also, avoid "broad" or unenforceable restrictions. Some libraries allow everyone to enter if they are "using the library materials." This broad restriction allows staff to ask those patrons not using materials found in the library to leave, but this can be quickly avoided by patrons pulling out an item and opening it in front of them. Then it becomes a judgment call by the librarian as to whether the patron is really "using" the material. Courts tend to lean toward the rights of patrons and such judgment calls could be very suspect.

Lastly, libraries must also consider the restrictions placed on federal depository libraries. Some form of access to federal documents must be allowed or the library could risk losing federal depository status.

Copyright versus Interlibrary Loan and Photocopiers

There have been no cases of patrons suing a library for access to information denied because of the copyright law. But the future is uncertain about whether libraries can be sued for allowing illegal access to copyrighted material requested by patrons (suits by publishers against libraries); or whether libraries can deny information due to copyright concerns (patrons suing the library for denial of information). For example:

What should librarians do when patrons state that they are taking out a videotape to copy at home?

What should a librarian do when a patron is photocopying an entire copyrighted book?

When the librarian is asked by a faculty member to borrow a copy of a copyrighted book on interlibrary loan and then photocopy it in its entirety for that professor?

The copyright laws were developed under the Copyright Revision Act of 1976 (17 USC Section 101, et seq.). Section 107 states the rule of "fair use" by specifying that the copying of material for purposes of "criticism, comment, news report, teaching (including multiple copies for classroom use), scholarship, or research is not an infringement of copyright."

Section 108 of the Copyright Revision Act discusses what libraries may copy. Section 108(a) states that:

> . . . it is not an infringement of copyright for a library or archives, or any of its employees acting within the scope of their employment, to reproduce no more than one copy . . . of a work, or to distribute such copy . . . if (1) the reproduction or distribution is made without any purpose of direct or indirect commercial advantage; (2) the collections of the library or archives are (i) open to the public, or (ii) available not only to researchers affiliated with the library or archives or with the institution of which it is a part, but also to other persons doing research in a specialized field; and (3) the reproduction or distribution of the work includes a notice of copyright.

What can the library do to protect itself from copyright suits? If the library believes that a patron may be illegally copying, the library should either inform the patron of the copyright law or refuse to allow the item (book or tape) to be used by the patron. The former action gives some protection to the library, but if the patron continues with the illegal copying, it might possibly be argued that the library allowed it to occur with knowledge of the patron's intent. There have been no cases in this area, but one person having knowledge of an illegal act has led courts in the past to infer participation in that act.

It should also be noted that librarians should not state to the patron that a specific act is not allowed, as this could be considered interpreting the Copyright Act and possibly the unauthorized practice of law. It would be best to state it in terms of the "possibility" of infringement and give the patron the Copyright Act to interpret for himself or herself (either verbally, or—better still—with the written provisions of the Copyright Act). As for the refusal to lend items because of the belief that they will be illegally copied—this practice, while totally protecting the library of any copyright infringement claims, could result in the patron arguing that the library made the wrong conclusion and had no right to prohibit the patron from using the information.

Equipment should be carefully monitored. If video and audio players are located in the library they should, for purposes of total copyright protection, allow for viewing or listening of tapes only, not for recording. As a rule, equipment should not be allowed to leave the library, where it is impossible to monitor usage. There should also be a limit on the number of patrons in a group which is viewing copyrighted videotapes in the library, unless they have met the exceptions of Section 110 of the Copyright Act.

Photocopiers present a similar problem. Section 108(f)(1) of the Copyright Act does state that libraries and their employees shall not be held liable for copyright infringement for the unsupervised use of reproducing equipment located in the library, provided that the equipment displays a notice that the making of the copy is subject to the copyright law. Each copier should have the copyright notice affixed to it or in another prominent place next to the copier. A notice could be similar to the following:

> Unauthorized copying of copyrighted material is prohibited under the United States Copyright Revision Act of 1976 (Title 17 USC).

It should be noted that this does not exempt copying handled by libraries and their staff. Libraries cannot get around the rule by allowing employees to use unsupervised photocopiers or other copy machines.

Interlibrary loan requests for photocopies are given exemptions from the Copyright Act. Requests can be filled for single articles or parts of other material if the copy becomes the property of the user for purposes of scholarship or research. A copyright warning must be prominently displayed both in the area where orders are received and on the order form (Sec. 108(d)).

A patron can also order a photocopy of an entire work or substantial part of a work if it cannot be obtained at a "fair price" and the above rules have been applied (Sec. 108(e)). What is important is that Section 108(d) and (e) do state that the library must first determine potential use through reasonable investigation and must have no knowledge or notice that the copy will be used for any purpose other than scholarship or research. Also, the library must reasonably investigate the possibility of buying the item, according to Section 108(e), before making a substantial or entire copy of a work.

Thus, a patron's request for an item must be considered very carefully when a photocopy is requested through interlibrary loan. Libraries can protect themselves from patrons requesting items or copies that cannot be obtained legally by doing the following: posting a copyright notice in prominent view where orders are received; having a patron complete or at least sign an interlibrary loan form that includes a copyright notice; adding a copyright notice to the copy (top page is prominent); and for patrons who still insist on copies that the library cannot legally obtain, giving them a copy of the pertinent USC sections. Faculty or administrative users of academic libraries must be treated the same as other patrons to protect libraries from suits by publishers or authors.

Reference Information

An important service in any library is assisting patrons in their search for information. But there is also a limitation that must be put on the librarian when patrons ask the librarian to go one step further and interpret the information. While libraries are faced with many subject fields that must be carefully handled, two fields are specifically mentioned here for their high importance and potential liability: the medical and legal fields.

Unless you are appropriately licensed in the state in which you are located, you may not practice law or medicine. There have been many cases where the courts have stated that giving out opinions derived from information, preparing documents, or even assisting patrons in analyzing information is an unauthorized practice.

Drawing the line between helping patrons find information and the unauthorized practice of law or medicine is important. The American Association of Law Libraries Code of Ethics requires librarians to avoid the unauthorized practice of law while providing access to legal information (*AALL Handbook* [1993–94] 691). There have also been prohibitions on the unauthorized practice of law in court (*Akron Bar Assn. v. Singleton*, 573 N.E.2d 1249 [1990], *State Bar v. Cramer*, 249 N.W.2d 1 [Mich. 1976]).

When there is a question as to whether some task constitutes the unauthorized practice of law or medicine, one should ask if the information is reference or if it is research or advice. A librarian may show a patron where specifically requested items are located but a librarian should not analyze or interpret the actual information for the patron. Going one step further, while a librarian could show a patron a particular index or form book and how to use the item, it must be the patron who actually opens up the item and locates the information. It is the patron who must use the materials in the library and it is the patron who must interpret cases, statutes, policies, and draft legal documents. One exception to this rule should be noted by prison librarians: assistance with preparation and filing of legal documents for prison inmates is allowed (*Bounds v. Smith*, 430 U.S. 817 [1977]).

This prohibition against assistance in these areas may not be understood by patrons. In many public libraries, patrons may need assistance with a medical or legal problem. They may state that they cannot afford a doctor or an attorney and so have come to the library. Librarians must continuously insist to such a patron that they are not refusing to help the patron, but they can only show the patron where the information is located. There has not been a case won by a patron who insisted that access to information was denied because a librarian refused to go further than to show where the information is located. However, there is the potential for liability when librarians step over the line, either by providing wrong or misunderstood information or giving out information, resulting in the patron being harmed. It also opens the door for legal action by the appropriate authorities (such as the police, American Medical Association, or American Bar Association, for example).

Some law librarians may have a law or medical degree and be authorized to practice. Libraries should still discourage legal or medical work while the staff member is working as a librarian. There is a risk of malpractice lawsuits against both the librarian and the library if the advice given is incorrect or misinterpreted.

Libraries can do several things to assist librarians in informing patrons about what staff can and cannot do:

1. Post a sign at the reference desk that states librarians will only provide access to legal and medical information and cannot supply advice.
2. Prepare pathfinders for specific areas of the law or medicine that list form books, indexes, loose-leaf services, and outside

legal or medical organizations (including telephone numbers) that could assist indigent patrons. The pathfinders can also give simple instructions on finding and reading cases and statutes or medical information.

3. Invest in self-help books, form books, and digests.

BIBLIOGRAPHY

ACCESS

Abrams, Robert H. and Donald J. Dunn. "The Law Library's Institutional Response to the Pro Se Patron: A Post-Faretta Review." *Western New England Law Review* 1 (1978):47.

Cogswell, Robert E. and Bardie C. Wolfe. "Hours of Opening and After-Hours Access in University Law Libraries." *Law Library Journal* 66 (1973):88.

Danner, Richard. "From the Editor: Public Access to the Law." *Law Library Journal* 79 (1987):163.

Johnson, Brenda L. "A Case Study in Closing the University Library to the Public." *College & Research Libraries News* 8 (1984):44.

Murray, James M. "Limiting Secondary Patrons' Use of Academic Law Libraries during Examination Periods." *Law Library Journal* 84 (1992): 365.

Snow, Barbara J. "When Goals Collide: Planning and Implementing a Restricted Access Policy at the University of Michigan Law Library." *Law Library Journal* 84 (1992):387.

COPYRIGHT

Heller, James S. "The Public Performance Right in Libraries: Is There Anything Fair about It?" *Law Library Journal* 84 (1992):315.

Tepper, Laurie C. "Copyright Law and Library Photocopying: An Historical Survey." *Law Library Journal* 84 (1992):341.

REFERENCE ISSUES

Berg, Robert T. "The Reference Librarian and the Pro Se Patron." *Law Library Journal* 69 (1976):26.

Brown, Yvette. "From the Reference Desk to the Jail House: Unauthorized Practice of Law and Librarians." *Legal Reference Services Quarterly* 13 (1994):31.

Chicco, Giuliano. "Ethics and Law Librarianship: A Panel Discussion." *Law Library Journal* 83 (1991):1.

Everett, John H. "Independent Information Professional and the Question of Malpractice Liability." *Online* 13 (May 1989):65.

Garner, Kathy. "Lawyer-Librarians in Public Law Schools: The Ethical Conundrums of Pro Bono Activities." *Law Library Journal* 84 (1992):31.

Herskowitz, Suzan. "Lawyer-Librarians in Public Law Schools: Too Many Unanswered Questions." *Law Library Journal* 85 (1993):205.

Kirkwood, C. C. and Tim J. Watts. "Legal Reference Service: Duties v. Liabilities." *Legal Reference Services Quarterly* 3 (1983):67.

Leone, Gerome. "Malpractice Liability of a Law Librarian?" *Law Library Journal* 73 (1980):44.

Mills, Robin. "Reference Service vs. Legal Advice: Is It Possible to Draw the Line?" *Law Library Journal* 72 (1979):179.

Pritchard, Teresa and Michelle Quigley. "The Information Specialist: A Malpractice Risk Analysis." *Online* 13 (May 1989):57.

Protti, Maria E. "Dispensing Law at the Front Lines: Ethical Dilemmas in Law Librarianship." *Library Trends* 40 (1991):234.

Rice, Michael E. "Reference Service Versus Unauthorized Legal Practice—Implications for the Canadian Reference Librarian." *Legal Reference Services Quarterly* 10 (1990):41.

Schanck, Peter G. "Unauthorized Practice of Law and the Legal Reference Librarian." *Law Library Journal* 72 (1979):57.

9

Sexual Harassment in the Library

Denise J. Johnson

In the June 1992 issue of *Wilson Library Bulletin,* Will Manley published a survey entitled "Librarians and Sex." What happened to Mr. Manley as a result of his article has become a footnote in library history.[1] An interesting offshoot is that, despite the fact that much of the survey was intended to be humorous, Manley did query those surveyed as to their experiences with sexual harassment. Seventy-eight percent of female respondents and seven percent of male respondents reported sexual harassment by a library patron. Another fourteen percent reported having been sexually harassed by a library supervisor or coworker.

Although Manley's survey was not conducted scientifically, the response to the harassment question amounted to a collective wake-up call to library administrators. Library workers, particularly in public libraries, are experiencing an unnecessarily stressful level of sexual harassment. Fortunately, there are steps that can be taken to mitigate the problems caused by this type of harassment.

In order to determine the best response to sexual harassment, it is first necessary to understand what actions constitute sexual harassment. Preventive measures, investigative procedures, and legal action can alleviate the problems associated with sexual harassment and make libraries safer and more comfortable working places. It is important to note that taking the necessary steps to assist employees with

Library administrators Matthew Kubiak, director of the Bloomington Public Library, Leann Johnson, assistant director of the Peoria Public Library, and Marsha Westfall, director of the Peoria Heights Public Library, generously gave their time and observations on the problems of sexual harassment of library staff by patrons.

problems of sexual harassment in the workplace is the employer's legal responsibility.

Defining Sexual Harassment

People define sexual harassment differently. Legal definitions differ from the definitions understood by the general public and members of special interest groups. While ethical, emotional, and moral discussions of sexual harassment may be interesting, the legal definitions are the most useful for our purposes.

The legal definition of sexual harassment has been interpreted by the United States Supreme Court in keeping with guidelines developed by the United States Equal Employment Opportunity Commission. Sexual harassment law is based on compliance with Title VII of the Civil Rights Act of 1964, which prohibits all forms of discrimination in employment on the basis of race, color, religion, national origin, or sex. The guidelines promulgated by the EEOC can be found in Title 29 of the Code of Federal Regulations, Section 1604. The EEOC's definition is as follows:

> (a) Harassment on the basis of sex is a violation of section 703 of title VII. Unwelcome sexual advances, requests for sexual favors, and other verbal or physical conduct of a sexual nature constitute sexual harassment when (1) submission to such conduct is made either explicitly or implicitly a term or condition of an individual's employment, (2) submission to or rejection of such conduct by an individual is used as the basis for employment decisions affecting such individual, or (3) such conduct has the purpose or effect of unreasonably interfering with an individual's work performance or creating an intimidating, hostile, or offensive working environment.[2]

Because the United States is a country in which laws are based on precedent, it is necessary to have some knowledge of the legal concepts concerning sexual harassment in order to fully comprehend the EEOC regulations. While most people understand the principles behind "quid pro quo" sexual harassment (for example, job benefits are exchanged for acceptance of sexual receptivity), there is considerable confusion over the "hostile environment" type of sexual harassment complaint. Much of the case law revolves around three issues: what constitutes the condition of "unwelcome" behavior, of what does a "hostile environment" consist, and whether the harassment is sexually discriminatory. The subtypes of sexual harassment have been divided into three categories: *visual*, *verbal*, and *physical* harassment. We will examine each of these concepts briefly.

Unwelcome Conduct

Unwelcome conduct sounds pretty easy to define. If I make a sexual suggestion or remark to someone and that person does not like the remark, it's unwelcome, right? Not necessarily. While it is true that unwelcome conduct has been defined as conduct that would be offensive or undesirable to a "reasonable person/woman," it is also necessary to show that the conduct was not encouraged or incited by the recipient.

The "unwelcome" conduct of behavior can be pretty tricky to determine. What happens, for instance, if someone routinely engages with others in consensual sexual banter or jokes, but subsequently decides such banter is no longer acceptable? As another example, what happens if two people are involved in a consensual sexual relationship, the relationship ends, and one of the people involved continues to pursue the relationship? Similar cases have been litigated. In such cases, the demeanor and verbal responses of recipients to the behavior have been deciding factors in the outcomes of the cases. While it is not always necessary for a recipient of harassing conduct to explicitly state that the conduct is unwelcome for it to be found so, there must be some observable indications that the conduct is unwelcome for such a finding to be made.

Hostile Environment

A hostile environment is one in which the victim(s) of sexually harassing conduct is subjected to a pervasive atmosphere of offensive conduct. It is not necessary for the conduct to be sexual for it to constitute sexual harassment. "As long as the harassment can be shown to be motivated by plaintiff's gender, assuming all other requirements are met, hostile environment sexual harassment will be found."[3] It is important to note that infrequent episodes of sexually harassing behavior may not be legally actionable, as long as prompt and appropriate action is taken by the employer.

Many people find the concept of a hostile environment very difficult to comprehend. This is particularly true in libraries where a strong emphasis is placed on freedom of expression and civil liberties. For some people the very presence of sexually explicit materials in a library's collection might seem to meet the definition of hostile environment. There are many stories of complaints of sexual harassment wherein the alleged perpetrator was reading a sexually oriented magazine or viewing a sexually oriented computer file in the presence of the complainant. In most cases, such behavior has not been construed as sexual harassment by the courts. If, however, the person viewing the sexually oriented materials does so pointedly (such as by opening out centerfolds in a very obvious manner, making comments or sounds in accompaniment) and does so repeatedly, such behavior could certainly be considered sexual harassment.

Sexual Discrimination

Complaints of harassment must be proved to be based on the recipient's gender in order to be considered sexual harassment under current law. In other words, for behavior to be considered sexual harassment, the behavior must be based on gender or gender stereotypes; the behavior itself need not be sexual in nature. Unfortunately, many people suffer harassment from supervisors, coworkers, or customers or patrons, but workers are not protected from generalized harassment under Title VII of the Civil Rights Act, unless the harassment is due to the recipient's race, color, religion, national origin, or sex.

Some victims of harassment consider that their gender makes the harassment sexual harassment, but such is not the case. Someone who is the office "whipping boy" or is often the butt of jokes due to personal idiosyncracies may certainly complain to his or her supervisor over the poor treatment, but sexual harassment is not at issue.

Subtypes of Sexual Harassment

There are various types of sexual harassment which are described in the following text.

Visual Harassment

Visual harassment includes such activities as leering, showing or displaying sexually oriented materials (for example, hanging up posters or calendars featuring nude or semi-nude people, tacking up sexually oriented cartoons), and placing sexually oriented materials where the recipient will find them (such as leaving sexually oriented jokes or cartoons on the recipient's desk or in the recipient's mailbox).

Verbal Harassment

Verbal harassment includes, but is not limited to, making sexually suggestive comments, remarking inappropriately on the recipient's appearance, persistently requesting dates or propositioning the recipient, and making stereotypical derogatory comments (for example, women are poor at math, women drivers, men are insensitive). If you are concerned that you may never again tell someone that you like their new dress, remember, the comments must be unwelcome and inappropriate to constitute harassment. It is fine to say "I like the color of that dress you're wearing." It is inappropriate to say, "Wow, your legs look sexy in that skirt."

Physical Harassment

Physical harassment includes such conduct as inappropriate touching, patting, brushing against, and physically blocking the recipient's exit. Some well-intentioned people are concerned that innocent gestures, such as patting someone on the arm or shoulder, will be misconstrued as sexual harassment. It should be noted that certain conditions must be met for behavior to be considered harassment; in addition to touching someone, the touch must be unwelcome, and it must be due to the recipient's sex for the behavior to be considered sexual harassment. It should also be noted that behavior must be *pervasive* to be considered harassment. Brushing against someone once in an elevator is not sexual harassment; brushing against someone at every opportunity is.

Patron Behavior and Employer Responsibility

Most of the literature concerning sexual harassment deals with the problems employees experience with coworkers and supervisors at work. There are a couple of reasons for this. The first is that the laws dealing with sexual harassment have to do with the civil rights of employees. While it might be considered sexually harassing behavior for a stranger on the street to make catcalls and sexual remarks, it is not feasible to sue such persons under Title VII of the Civil Rights Act. The second reason is that employers have limited responsibility for the behavior of persons not employed by them. There are, however, some circumstances under which employers are liable for behavior by clients, patrons, or customers.

Sexual harassment by persons not under the employer's direct control, or third party sexual harassment, is considered by some legal specialists to be the "new frontier in sexual discrimination."[4] Typically, third party sexual harassment has been ignored as being "part of the job" or "just the way things are." It has not been uncommon for waitresses to be given revealing uniforms to wear and told to expect lewd comments and ogling by customers. Women working in sales positions have reported that their persons were considered part of the purchase by some customers. Many public service workers, such as the frontline staff members in libraries, experience similar situations and problems.

In the conversations this author has had with administrators from public libraries and in studying the library literature, the types of complaints regarding patrons are both similar and unsettling. Workers complain of being leered at, stared at, propositioned, and brushed against. They complain of having their personal space violated and of fearing that those who leer by day will become stalkers at closing time. Sometimes patrons began encounters with innocent questions, and when they received positive, friendly responses from the worker, they took those responses as invitations to converse in a much more personal manner. One such patron, on being treated humanely by a library staffer, escalated his behavior from bothersome chattiness to personal questions and finally to notes filled with sexual innuendo before the library was able to document the behavior, and thus stop the harasser. In another case, a five-year library employee who was known for her "good people skills" became so unnerved by the persistent problems of patron sexual harassment she encountered in her work that she quit her job in the library. All of this is especially incongruous when paired with the fact that many people choose to work in libraries because they are perceived as safe and quiet places to work.

On a positive note, at least the people mentioned here did complain. Persons subjected to third party sexual harassment often do not complain, either because they fear for their jobs or they do not want to be considered incapable of handling their work. After all, the third parties involved are often customers, and most businesses are extremely wary of offending customers. Some library workers who have endured sexual harassment without complaint cite such reasons as the failure by administrators to act on previous complaints, administrative inability to deal with sexual harassment, fear of being blamed for instigating harassing behavior, and fear of being labeled a troublemaker. For many library workers, such fears are not unfounded. It is the responsibility of library administrators and supervisors to assure workers that their concerns and complaints will not be met with reprisals or dismissal.

The boundaries of employer responsibility for third party sexual harassment are still being defined by the courts, but there are measures that will both mitigate the problems employees face in such situations and help assure that employers responsibly address employee complaints. The next section deals with these measures.

Preventing and Stopping Sexual Harassment in the Library

Most of the information on sexual harassment indicates that the most effective way to stop sexual harassment is to prevent it from taking place. However, prevention practices are more likely to work with internal sexual harassment problems than with third party sexual harassment. But the procedures used can help the victims of harassing behavior better understand their situations and develop coping skills. Some of the procedures recommended for preventing sexual harassment will also help curb other problem behaviors and prevent the repetition of sexual harassment.

It is unlikely that sexual harassment will become an anachronism within the next few years, but libraries that adopt proactive measures will improve workplace safety, security, and comfort while helping to indemnify the library against costly legal entanglements.

Sexual Harassment Policies

The first step in combatting sexual harassment is to develop an explicit, formal, written policy. The policy should be widely distributed and prominently posted. The policy or a reminder about the policy should be redistributed at least twice yearly. The policy must not be just a piece of paper. A policy that is too vague or not enforced offers no protection to workers or employers.

Elements of an effective library policy on sexual harassment include

- a definition of sexual harassment
- a statement on the library's philosophy regarding sexual harassment
- a notice that persons reporting sexual harassment will not suffer reprisals
- examples of prohibited conduct
- procedures for reporting sexual harassment (including the names or job titles of persons to whom recipients of harassing behavior should report the behavior)
- penalties for misconduct under the policy
- procedures for investigating and resolving complaints
- procedures for education and training regarding the policy and sexual harassment.

While not all legally acceptable policies on sexual harassment contain all of these elements, these are the key elements included in a court-ordered policy adopted after a case wherein the company's policy was held to be inadequate.[5] Among the benefits of such an explicit policy is that workers are no longer in the dark about their rights and responsibilities, and administrators have strong guidelines for developing procedures. (For materials on developing policies, consult the bibliography at the end of this chapter.)

Procedures for Handling Sexual Harassment Complaints

Choose Someone to Investigate the Complaint

All complaints of sexual harassment, even if they are not called sexual harassment by the complainant, must be treated seriously and responded to promptly. A member of the library staff should be designated to investigate complaints of sexual harassment. Who that person may be will depend on the size of your library, the nature of the complaint, and any personal factors which might influence the investigation (such as a close relationship between the investigator and the complainant or between the investigator and the alleged harasser).

In most cases, the person designated to investigate sexual harassment complaints will be the library's personnel administrator, the assistant director, director, or the supervisor of the complainant. Some flexibility in designating an investigator is necessary to assure an objective investigation. If the person usually designated is a close personal friend of the complainant or has had substantial problems with the complainant in the past, an alternate investigator should be appointed. Similarly, if the investigator has personal ties to the alleged harasser, either negative or positive, an alternate investigator should be chosen.

Since the person investigating complaints of sexual harassment requires some training, there should be more than one staff member trained, if possible.

Act Promptly

It is important to investigate complaints of sexual harassment promptly. An investigation of a complaint should begin within a day or two of the complaint. Inasmuch as possible, the investigation should be completed within two weeks of the complaint. Appropriate measures to resolve the complaint should be taken as promptly as possible. Some complaints can be investigated and resolved within a very short period of time, for example as when a patron is publicly abusive; the supervisor is notified, the police are called, and the patron is banned from entering the library—all within an hour or two. At other times, complaints may be of more subtle behavior, requiring some record-keeping and further investigation before corrective actions can be taken. In all cases, investigation and resolution must be as prompt as possible. Swift action helps to make the workplace more harmonious, engenders employee confidence in supervisors and administrators, and lessens legal liability.

Conduct the Investigation

The person investigating a sexual harassment complaint needs to talk with anyone who might have knowledge of the incident or incidents. Frequently, victims of sexual harassment are embarrassed by the situation in which they find themselves and might prefer that all matters be kept confidential. The investigator should exercise caution in making statements to the victim and to any witnesses. While it is possible to limit the number of people who need to know about an incident and keep details confidential, strict confidentiality may not ensure a thorough investigation or may prevent eventual legal processes. A generally acceptable guide is for the investigator to tell people information that will be shared only with those who need to know.

Sexual harassment can be a very emotional issue, so it is important that the investigator remains objective and keeps discussions on target. While it is natural for people to want to gossip or engage in speculation, the person investigating the complaint needs to maintain focus. Staff members who are involved in the situation or who need to be questioned should be encouraged to maintain a business-like attitude regarding incidents of sexual harassment. Joking and speculating may release tension for some staff members but may be hurtful to the complainant. By remaining focused, the investigator helps to create an environment more conducive to resolving the problem.

Get the Information in Writing

The investigator will need to keep a written record of what is said by each person interviewed. Any notes kept by the people involved (such as the complainant and the supervisor) should also be part of the record. A written report of the incident(s) with any such evidentiary notes should be kept on file. Written records can prove beneficial should there be repercussions as a result or recurrences of offensive behavior.

Investigators will need to elicit certain facts from the complainant. The first thing that needs to be determined is exactly what took place. If, for instance, the complaint is that a patron has been staring at the complainant all day, it would be useful to include some details in the written report, such as when the complainant first noticed the patron, how long the patron has been in the vicinity, and the duration of the staring. If the complaint concerns a pattern of behavior, rather than a specific incident, the report should include the number of times the complainant has experienced the objectionable behavior and any notes that have been kept to record repetitive minor problems. Any notes or pictures given to the complainant by the patron should also be included in the file.

The report should include any actions taken by the complainant to let the offending patron know the behavior was unwelcome, whether the action was verbal (asking the patron to stop the offensive behavior) or non-verbal (turning away, walking away, showing distress). Clearly, some of the abusive behavior engaged in by some library patrons would be unwelcome to anyone. It will not be necessary to prove that staff members find loud, obscene language or flashing unwelcome in order to get the police to take action. For some of the more subtle forms of abusive behavior, however, evidence of this nature may prove helpful in controlling it or in prosecuting offenders.

Retaliation against Complainants

Staff who complain about sexual harassment *must* be assured that they will not be retaliated against in any way for making a complaint even if the complaint does not turn out to be valid. Two people experiencing the same set of events may have radically differing views of what occurred.

When investigating a sexual harassment complaint, it may be determined that no harm was intended by the subject of the complaint and that the behavior was misunderstood. Some patrons may suffer from a physical ailment which makes them appear to be glaring or staring, when they are in fact just sitting quietly or possibly even experiencing seizure-related problems. Patrons with disorders such as Tourette's Syndrome may have physical spasms or shout out words or unintelligible sounds, which could be misinterpreted by staff members unfamiliar with such disorders or with the patron.

The important thing for staff members to know is that they should feel free to make their concerns known, without fear of retaliation. It is the responsibility of the employer and the courts to determine whether an act or series of actions constitutes sexual harassment. As long as the employee makes the complaint in good faith, the employee is legally protected from retaliation by the employer. Administrators should be aware that transferring a complainant to a less desirable position is considered a form of retaliation. Only false complaints made with malice or revenge as a motive should be subject to disciplinary action.

Complainant Expectations

Finally, the complainant should be asked what outcome is desired as a result of the complaint. For example: does he or she want a supervisor, a security guard, or a law officer to speak to the offending patron? The patron barred from the library temporarily or permanently? Is he or she willing to press charges if the offense is serious enough to warrant legal intervention? The action taken should be appropriate to the offense, and the complainant should be made aware of what type of actions are available for the reported offense.

Library Responses to Sexual Harassment by Patrons

The methods libraries use to deal with offensive behavior by patrons vary in accordance with internal library procedures, local laws, and local law enforcement agencies. In libraries where a good relationship with the local police department exists, there is often a great deal of positive support for keeping miscreants out of the library and assistance in dealing with more threatening patrons. Often, less drastic measures can be effectively used to halt or prevent staff sexual harassment by patrons.

Responding to Complaints of Non-threatening Behavior

One of the most pervasive aspects of sexual harassment is that it is so common and frequent that many people do not recognize their behavior as offensive or as harassment. Our culture is one in which, not so many years ago, comments now considered harassment were once considered complimentary, humorous, or at the least, insignificant. Many people are still operating under codes of behavior that were formerly acceptable.

Since such people usually do not have harmful intentions toward others, it can be quite effective to simply tell them that their behavior is offensive. Within the literature on sexual harassment and this author's discussions with others, notification that behavior is offensive has been cited as among the most effective means of preventing and arresting sexual harassment. If the staff member does not feel comfortable telling the offender that his or her behavior is bothersome, a supervisor or administrator can do so.

Handling Complaints of Repetitive or Threatening Behavior

When the initial actions taken have not stopped a persistent harasser, or when the initial complaint is of a serious nature, it is necessary to increase the level of response by the library administration. For patrons who repeatedly engage in milder forms of harassment (for example, staring, making suggestive comments, displaying sexually oriented print or pictorial materials), a written warning from the library administrator, a discussion of the possible legal repercussions of actions with either a library security officer or a law officer, or limited banishment from the library may suffice to halt the harassment.

For more serious offenses, or when other methods have not worked, it will be necessary to involve law enforcement officials. Since laws vary from place to place, administrators will need to be aware of the laws and regulations in their area for local law enforcement personnel. Generally, the police will dispatch an officer to escort offenders from the building. They may ask whether the harassed individual wants to press charges for assault, or they may ask whether the library administration wants to press charges for disorderly conduct. In the interests of assuring the safety of library employees, the administration may want to adhere to a policy of pressing charges for disorderly conduct, even if the individual staff member(s) involved does not personally wish to press charges.

In some cases it may be necessary to file for a *restraining order*, barring the person from entering the library, loitering around library property, and accosting library staff members when they are not in the library. While restraining orders, in and of themselves, do not stop people from engaging in prohibited behavior, they do make it possible for charges of criminal trespass to be filed against repeat offenders. Library staff can be alerted to be on the lookout for such persons, so that the police may be called immediately should they attempt to return to the library. Library administrators, particularly in public libraries where policies may need library board approval, will be well-served to have procedures spelled out in advance for various types of potential problems. In academic libraries, such policies may be established by the larger institution.

When Staff Keeps Silent

Library staff members sometimes resist notifying patrons that their behavior is offensive or reporting it to supervisors because they do not wish to offend the patron. However, there are times when speaking up is imperative.

If someone repeatedly behaves or speaks in a manner that is degrading or embarrassing, it is important to let that person know how this behavior affects others. If the behavior of patrons in the library makes you feel as though you don't want to go to work, you are afraid to leave the building, you'd like to change jobs, or you are beginning to suffer from physical illness due to stress, then you need to tell someone about the behavior. If you elect to tell the offending person directly, note what happened—when and what you said—so that there is a record if the behavior is repeated. If you do not feel able to confront the patron directly for whatever reason, tell the supervisor or someone in a position of authority in the library so the problem can be dealt with.

If, as a supervisor, you don't know whether the people you supervise are being subjected to offensive behavior, find out. We know that sexual harassment is a problem in public service organizations. We also know that employees are reluctant to report problems. However, it is important to remember that employers are legally responsible for failing to make necessary changes in work situations if there is *constructive knowledge* of sexual harassment. Constructive knowledge means the employer knew or should have known of sexual harassment problems. So, while supervisors and administrators may be feeling safe from possible claims of sexual harassment, they should be aware that the responsibility for reporting problems is not solely that of the victim.

A variety of measures can be taken to find out if there is a sexual harassment problem in your library, and if so, how large the problem is. Surveying staff anonymously may help uncover problems people are reluctant to discuss. You may want to hold a staff meeting wherein sexual harassment by patrons is the featured topic of discussion. Establishing a committee or charging an existing personnel committee to investigate staff concerns and recommend actions effectively encourages staff involvement. How the problem is approached is of less importance than that it *is* approached. Research indicates that in any but the smallest of libraries the administrators are usually surprised to learn the extent of the harassment experienced by staff.

Training Staff to Prevent and Respond to Sexual Harassment

Providing staff members with training will help them become more adept at preventing and responding to sexual harassment. A necessary component of an effective program is notifying staff members of library policies regarding sexual harassment and the interpretation of these policies. Staff members who regularly attend staff development training sessions will be less likely to fear lodging a complaint or getting help when they experience problems.

Where there are significant problems, administrators may want to hold sessions bi-annually regarding procedures and communications skills for dealing with sexual harassment. In libraries where these problems are less significant, sexual harassment coping skills and procedures can be components of training programs on general patron relations. These meetings may be held annually or even less frequently if the staff composition is stable.

The components of a library staff's training on sexual harassment should include

a clear definition of sexual harassment

a discussion of employee rights and responsibilities regarding sexual harassment

a discussion of the library's policies regarding sexual harassment

information concerning procedures for reporting complaints of sexual harassment

information regarding probable legal or disciplinary actions to be taken in the event that a complaint is filed

communications and coping skills for staff members subject to harassment from patrons.

Most of the training components should be covered in the library's policy on sexual harassment. Discussing them during a staff development or training workshop will ensure that staff are aware of the policies and that the administration considers sexual harassment an important subject. Communications and coping skills may be similar to the skills used in any other situation dealing with unpleasant patron behavior, but it is often helpful to discuss possible scenarios to ensure that staff are better prepared to deal with them.

Among the communications skills recommended for coping with sexual harassment is *assertiveness*. We may reject common stereotypes of library workers, while recognizing that some temperamental similarities are found among people who choose to work in libraries and in public service positions in general. Many people choose to work in libraries due to a desire to work in a "helping profession." Some people also choose to work in libraries because they see them as quiet, intellectually oriented places to work. Many such persons are often not assertive in their interpersonal relations and may experience more problems with troublesome patrons than would persons with less gentle personalities. Additionally, public service personnel are trained to be approachable which makes them even likelier targets for poorly socialized patrons.

In addition to assertiveness training, staff members may find it useful to attend training sessions on active listening and on dealing with angry, upset, or irate customers. While the situations discussed in this type of training are not exactly the same as those encountered in a sexual harassment situation, the skills taught would be valuable for anyone experiencing difficulties with patrons.

Typically, communications skills workshops will help staff members learn to communicate without "pushing peoples' buttons," to deflect or head off angry confrontations, and to express discomfort without engendering anger or becoming emotional. Having practiced responses to unacceptable behavior from patrons is helpful when situations do arise.

Legal Consequences of Inaction

Employers found to be in violation of sexual harassment law are liable under federal law only for actual losses and expenses suffered by the complainant. However, some losses may not be immediately recognized by employers. For example, a staff member who quits his or her job due to sexual harassment may be considered to have been "constructively fired" under the law, particularly if the employer did not take steps to prevent or stop sexual harassment. If the staff member then files a complaint against the employer, damages could include lost wages and any expenses incurred for counseling. Employers making good faith efforts to prevent or arrest workplace sexual harassment are viewed much more sympathetically by the courts.

State laws vary regarding awards for punitive damages. Library administrators need to make themselves and their governing bodies aware of state laws and regulations regarding sexual harassment.

Conclusions

Sexual harassment of library staff members by patrons is a bigger problem than most people recognize. The best defenses against legal liability are good policies and procedures to prevent and arrest sexual harassment in the workplace. Important defenses also include knowledge, policy setting, and staff training. In libraries where administrators take a proactive and positive stance against sexual harassment, employees will be empowered to work more effectively, safely, and comfortably. Library administrators who choose to ignore or denigrate the seriousness of workplace sexual harassment do so at their own peril and at the library's peril.

NOTES

1. As a result of the publication, Manley was fired by *Wilson Library Bulletin*'s editor, Leo Weins. Weins further ordered that all unsold copies of the offending issue of *Wilson Library Bulletin* be destroyed. Will Manley's WLB column was given residence in *American Libraries,* under the new rubric, "Will's World."

2. 29 CFR 1604.11.

3. Dawn D. Bennett-Alexander, "Hostile Environment Sexual Harassment: A Clearer View," *Labor Law Journal* 42 (March 1991):131–43.

4. Kathleen Murray, "Fighting Sexual Harassment Goes beyond Co-Workers, to Clients," *Washington Post,* Feb. 28, 1993, p.H2.

5. Dana S. Connell, "Effective Sexual Harassment Policies: Unexpected Lessons from Jacksonville Shipyards," *Employee Relations Law Journal* 17 (Autumn 1991):191–206.

Bibliography

American Library Association. Committee on the Status of Women in Librarianship. *Sexual Harassment in the Workplace.* Chicago: American Library Assn., 1988. (Available by request from ALA, 50 E. Huron St., Chicago, IL 60601.)

———. *Suggested Model for Addressing Sexual Harassment Issues in Libraries.* Chicago: American Library Assn., 1990. (Also available by request from ALA.)

Bovet, Susan. "Sexual Harassment: What's Happening and How to Deal with It." *Public Relations Journal* 49 (Nov. 1993): 26–29.

International Labour Office. "Combating Sexual Harassment at Work." *Conditions of Work Digest* 11 (1992): 1–300.

Peterson, Donald J. and Douglas P. Massengill. "Sexual Harassment Cases Five Years after Meritor Savings Bank v. Vinson." *Employee Relations Law Journal* 18 (Winter 1992): 489–515.

Simon, Howard A. "Ellison v. Brady: A 'Reasonable Woman' Standard for Sexual Harassment." *Employee Relations Law Journal* 17 (Summer 1991): 71–80.

Wagner, Ellen J. *Sexual Harassment in the Workplace: How to Prevent, Investigate, and Resolve Problems in Your Organization.* New York: AMACOM, 1992.

Winokur, L. A. "Workplace: Harassment of Workers by 'Third Parties' Can Lead into Maze of Legal, Moral Issues." *Wall Street Journal,* Oct. 26, 1992, p.B1.

10

Sexual Behavior in Libraries

Denise J. Johnson

There is very little information in the literature of library security regarding the problems experienced by library staff when their facilities become active sites for sexual assignations. Yet, this is not an uncommon problem in libraries. It is not just to keep the homeless and indigent from using restrooms as shower rooms that so many public libraries restrict or regulate access to their public restrooms. Sexual activity in public buildings and facilities is a problem for many libraries, and it is a problem best allayed through preventive measures.

Most reported public sexual activity is homosexual activity, with the public restroom serving as a meeting place for people who do not know one another. There have been some reports of inappropriate public sexual activity by heterosexuals, although such activity is usually reported as only occasional. There have also been some reports of sexual activities taking place in libraries (particularly on college campuses) as a thrill-seeking activity, similar to sexual activity in airplanes, elevators, and other unusual locations. Such reports are generally anecdotal, possibly because the subject does not seem worthy of reportage or because libraries would rather not publicize the fact.

While occasional or thrill-seeking types of sexual activities are likely to cause embarrassment and distress for both the participants and the library staff member confronted by the activities, the methods used for dealing with other types of inappropriate library behavior will probably suffice for sexually inappropriate behavior. In public libraries, such measures may include asking the offenders to leave the library, prohibiting offenders from using the library for a period of time, or in particularly blatant cases, filing disorderly conduct charges with the local law enforcement authorities. Similar measures are likely to be used by university libraries, with the more excessive cases being referred to the campus judicial system or to campus security or police officers.

"Tearoom" Behavior Problems

The problems faced by a library where a restroom or other isolated areas have become sexual gathering places are far more difficult to deal with than those associated with isolated or occasional incidences of inappropriate public sexual behavior. Most library workers are unfamiliar with the phenomenon of "tearoom" sexual behavior, even though libraries may frequently be the sites for such behavior. The following quotation from Laud Humphrey's seminal sociological study on the subject explains the phenomenon.

> According to its most precise meaning in the argot, the only "true" tearoom is one that gains a reputation as a place where homosexual encounters occur. Presumably, any restroom could qualify for this distinction, but comparatively few are singled out for this function at any one time. For instance, I have researched a metropolitan area with more than ninety public toilets in its parks, only twenty of which are in regular use as locales for sexual games. . . .
>
> Public restrooms are chosen by those who want homoerotic activity without commitment for a number of reasons. They are accessible, easily recognized by the initiate, and provide little public visibility.[1]

Library workers generally become aware that some area of the building is being used as a sexual tearoom when activities reach such a level that evidence is ubiquitous. Some of the signals to watch for include suggestive graffiti, used tissues and condoms, notes, excessive and repetitive use of restroom facilities, and even alterations in the physical structure of toilet stalls (for example, the construction of "glory holes").

Discouraging "Tearoom" Behavior in Libraries

Several methods have proved useful in discouraging the use of library facilities for tearoom sex. Frequent inspections of restroom facilities by staff members or security officers is a useful preventive measure. Installing security cameras near entrances to secluded restrooms or stack areas is another useful safeguard. Keeping graffiti cleaned off or painted over, removing notes and other evidence of prohibited activities, and making changes to the layout of restrooms to provide less accommodation for interactions are all useful control mechanisms. It is important to note that once an area has become favored as a sexual hangout, continued vigilance will be necessary to halt ongoing activities.

In libraries where no such activities have taken hold, it is possible to prevent them altogether using forethought. In smaller libraries regulating access to restrooms may prove to have sufficient deterrent effects. In larger libraries, placing security cameras near secluded and low-traffic areas is a helpful deterrent. Frequent but randomly timed maintenance and cleaning schedules will make restrooms less attractive gathering places.

In designing or remodeling library buildings, entrances to restrooms should be placed where they are clearly visible from library service points. For aesthetic reasons, architects often prefer recessed or concealed entrances to restrooms. Convincing the architect to make restroom entrances readily visible will not only help to prevent unauthorized and unwanted use of the library facilities but may help decrease the number of times the reference librarian is asked for directions in finding the restroom.

NOTE

1. Laud Humphries, *Tearoom Trade: Impersonal Sex in Public Places,* enlarged ed. (New York: Aldine, 1975), 2–3.

BIBLIOGRAPHY

Delph, Edward W. "Preventing Public Sex in Library Settings." *Library & Archival Security* 3 (Summer 1980): 17–26

———. *The Silent Community: Public Homosexual Encounters.* Beverly Hills: Sage, 1978.

Gray, Jane Karen. "The Tearoom Revisited: A Study of Impersonal Homosexual Encounters in a Public Setting." Ph.D. diss., Ohio State University, 1988.

Reddy, Deepika. "Wherever the Mood Strikes You." *U. Magazine* (Aug. 1994): 14. First published in the Penn State U. *Daily Collegian.*

III

What Are the Solutions?

11

Active Listening: Alleviating Patron Problems through Communication

Nathan M. Smith

If you worked at a reference desk for only a day, it is likely that you would encounter someone you would call a "problem patron." What is a problem patron? What librarians consider problem behavior can take many forms. For instance, this author recalls a student who was in my reference class many years ago. The way he dressed suggested he was a free thinker and a social activist. He worked at the time as a student reference assistant at the social science reference desk. During one of our class sessions, while talking about problem patrons, he told of a male patron who used the term "nigger." Knowing this had offended him, I asked, "How did you handle it?" and he replied, "I got rid of him as quickly as I could by telling him to use some encyclopedia. Later I saw him coming back and I hid in the office."

A patron's offensive words are just one example of problems a reference librarian may encounter. Other patrons may yell, swear, criticize, demand, harass, smell, or may just be generally obnoxious. However, the tenth patron to ask the same question is often considered a problem patron. In this case, it's *not* that the patron is a problem, it's that we get upset in repeating the same information ten times.

Active Listening

Determining problem ownership is a key factor in active listening. In order to use active listening, which means to hear and respond to the meaning and feeling behind a person's words, we must first determine *who owns the problem.* Is it the patron's problem or is it our own? If the patron's behavior interferes with our doing business (for example, breaking library rules or the law), then we own a problem. When we own a problem, we must not use active listening but must be assertive. If the patron owns the problem, however, then active listening is appropriate and will, in most cases, improve the communication and relationship. Active listening will be illustrated later, but first we need to understand problem ownership.

The Librarian Owns the Problem

Determining problem ownership can be difficult for some people and in some situations. The following are examples in which the librarian clearly owns a problem:

Patron is destroying library property

Patron is threatening to harm another patron or librarian

Patron is exhibiting himself

Patron is breaking library rules by:
- sleeping in the library
- eating or drinking in the library
- being loud and disturbing others
- not returning library material by the date due.

Patron Owns the Problem

In the following examples the patron owns a problem:

Patron is critical of the librarian or the library

Patron is impatient while waiting in line

Patron thinks a book should be banned

Patron thinks he or she should not have to pay a fine.

In cases where the patron owns the problem, active listening is appropriate, and it is probably the most helpful thing the librarian can do to ease the situation. Note that criticism is direct or implied in each of the four cases listed.

Handling Criticism

Critical patrons are often our greatest challenge and stressor. Most of us do not respond well to criticism. Critics make us nervous, our stomachs get upset, and our adrenalin runs rampant. If we see a patron coming who was previously critical of us or the library, we often get nervous and avoid the person.

A little insight into the behavior of the criticizing patron can eliminate or at least reduce the tension. Remember not to take the patron's criticism personally, because your critics are *not* describing you, although they want you to think they are. Critics' statements describe what they like and want. For example a female patron says, "Why can't you librarians ever make things simple? It is impossible to find anything using your computer catalog." It sounds like personal criticism, but it really says this patron is feeling frustrated.

Let's analyze the statement. First, note that it contains two of the infamous "you" statements that make most people feel criticized and defensive. "You" statements are often negative evaluations and put the sting in the statement. Second, the patron makes the statement angrily, which adds power to the sting. Anger is the most evident feeling and what most of us notice. The anger combined with the "you" statements make this a biting criticism—just what the patron intended. Anger is the secondary emotion.

Preceding the anger is another feeling. What is it? This is where we do our active listening. We have to *guess* at the underlying emotion, and there are several possibilities about what the feeling could be. It may be frustration. Another possibility is the patron is thinking, "I don't have much time and this is taking what little time I have," or she could be thinking, "I know about computers and this library system should follow the computer rules I know but, because they don't, it is frustrating me." It is also possible that she fears computers because they make her feel incompetent and she hates feeling that way.

Let's assume that frustration is our guess because it is safer to say, "You must feel quite frustrated by our computers." One cannot say "You feel incompetent in using the computer"; nor will it work to say "Sounds like you are afraid of computers."

Once we recognize that the patron is frustrated, we can see that the criticism is not about us. We can ignore it for a minute and use active listening to let her know we "hear" her. Often the active listening statement, "You sound as if you are very frustrated by our computers" is enough to drain away her anger. She might say, "Yeah. I really hate it when something that should be faster than the old card catalog takes three times as long."

Notice the active listening statement, "You sound as if you are very frustrated by our computers," is our attempt to reflect the primary emotion or feeling we are hearing rather than the secondary emotion—anger. It may work if you said, "You sound like you are very angry about our computer system," but it could also lead to continued anger. Since the patron already has her adrenalin flowing, she may say, "You're damned right I am!" If she did, you could still continue active listening by recognizing the emotion and say, "I can see that. Tell me what is it that bothers you most." This puts the emphasis on the problem—the computer's user friendliness—rather than on the librarian.

Using active listening and focusing on the problem will probably reduce the anger. If instead of continuing to actively listen, however, we had said, "Well, none of our other patrons have complained" (while thinking, "What is wrong with you, stupid?"), we should be prepared to receive the patron's next angry volley.

Let's suppose for a minute that the patron's criticism is valid: instructions on how to use the computer catalog are not clear. This is a systems mistake. Systems are created by humans and humans make mistakes. But remember, "mistake" is not a four-letter word. A mistake indicates a situation that needs to be corrected. Now that the patron has brought the problem to our attention, we can correct it and remove the frustration for future patrons.

Problem Patrons—More Examples

In order to get examples of problem patrons, the author conducted an informal, nonscientific survey of eight reference librarians and assistants in the Lee Library at Brigham Young University. I asked them, "What is a problem patron?" Each had immediate examples of patrons who frustrate and agitate them. Their thought was, "If these patrons would disappear from the earth, my job would be much easier." Most library workers will empathize with those surveyed and with their feelings about these particular problem patrons.

The following are just a few of the survey replies. Criticism of the librarian is present in all of them, although it may not be explicit. In each example the patron owns the problem, but the librarians' feelings regarding these patrons indicate the librarians have taken ownership. Each example is followed first by an analysis of the patron's criticism and the possible primary feeling, a typical response or responses, and then one or more active listening responses. In most cases, the typical response does not improve the situation and often makes it worse, because the patron feels unheard or confronted and criticized.

PROBLEM

Rude patrons who don't want to wait their turn. They get impatient and it shows.

Implied criticism:	You must be incompetent or you wouldn't be so slow.
Patron's primary feeling:	Frustration, anxiety
Typical staff response:	Looks at patron who is in line and says, "I'll be right with you," then when patron's turn comes (if he is still there) says, "May I help you?" (This is said coolly: response ignores the feeling.)
Active listening response:	Looks at patron who is in line and says, "I'll be right with you," then when patron's turn comes says, "I could see you were having a hard time waiting for me to get to you. Waiting in lines can be really frustrating. Now what can I do to help you?"

PROBLEM

Patron wants you to find the information for him or her, particularly on the computer.

Implied criticism:	You should show more concern: you're inconsiderate and unfeeling.
Patron's primary feeling:	Scared, frustrated, anxious, bewildered
Typical response:	"Try this and then let me know if you still need help."
Active listening response:	"I know that computers really frustrate some people. Let me repeat the steps for you one more time, then I need to get back to the desk. If you need more help later, let me know."

PROBLEM

Phone caller wants you to leave the desk and get the information for him.

Implied criticism:	I am a taxpayer, and you should help me just as much as someone who is in the library. Why are you so inconsiderate? Lazy?
Patron's primary feeling:	Frustrated, inconvenienced

Typical response:	"We simply don't have enough people to give indepth phone service. If you'll come to the library, we'll be glad to help you."
Active listening response:	"I know it must be frustrating to you and seem like an inconvenience to have to come down to the library for the information you need, but we simply don't have enough people to give in-depth phone service. If you'll come to the library, we'll be glad to help you."

PROBLEM

Patron gets upset when you must refer him to another reference desk.

Implied criticism:	You are just like all the rest of the bureaucrats: you don't know anything, so we get the runaround.
Patron's primary feeling:	Frustrated, worried, concerned
Typical response:	"The information you need is only found in the government documents section."
Active listening response:	"Sounds as if you are worried about getting the runaround again. Let me call the government documents section to let them know you are coming."

PROBLEM

Patron blames the reference librarian when it takes cataloging a long time to release a document.

Implied criticism:	If it is in the library, it should be available for checking out.
Patron's primary feeling:	Disappointed, frustrated
Typical response:	"It's not our fault. We can't do anything until cataloging releases it," or "It takes time to catalog—perhaps there is something else that will work for you."
Active listening response:	"I know it is frustrating. It frustrates me too because I like to give patrons what they need."

PROBLEM

Patron brings incomplete information to library from her teacher and refuses to believe the teacher could be wrong.

Implied criticism:	If you were a competent librarian, I could get the information I need.
Patron's primary feeling:	Frustrated
Typical response:	"Are you sure you copied it right?"
Active listening response:	"I'll bet you are feeling very frustrated; I know I am. Let's call your instructor and verify the reference."

PROBLEM

Patron is upset because the article he found in the index is one the library doesn't have, and it will take three or four weeks to get it through interlibrary loan.

Implied criticism:	Why don't you have what is in the indexes? It is not fair of you to get our hopes up and then let us down. You must not be a very good librarian.
Patron's primary feeling:	Frustrated, disappointed, anxious
Typical response:	"This is a national index, not one we produce locally; therefore, it indexes some journals that our library does not have. I can check to see if the University of Utah has what you want."
Active listening response:	"Sounds as if you are pretty disappointed. This situation comes up often and it always frustrates and challenges me. This is a national index, not one we produce locally; therefore, it indexes some journals that our library does not have. I can check to see if another university has what you want on inter-library loan."

Conclusion

Active listening improves interpersonal relationships and reduces tension. Active listening is accomplished by first recognizing that the other person owns the problem and then reflecting back to the person the primary feeling that we think we are hearing. It requires that we become skillful at not buying someone's problem and that we become adept at recognizing primary feelings. This last part is the more difficult part for most Americans, because many of us were taught not to express feelings. Parents often told us, "If you aren't quiet, I'll give you something to really cry about," or "Big boys (or girls) don't cry," or "You shouldn't feel that way." Since we were taught to not express feelings, most of us will have to practice recognizing someone's primary feeling. It is definitely worth the effort, however, because of the improved relationships, reduced personal stress, and increased job satisfaction.

BIBLIOGRAPHY

Gordon, Thomas. *P.E.T.: Parent Effectiveness Training*. New York: Peter H. Wyden, 1970.

Smith, Nathan M. and Irene Adams. "Using Active Listening to Deal with Patron Problems." *Public Libraries* 30 (July/Aug. 1991):236–39.

——— and Stephen D. Fitt. "Active Listening at the Reference Desk." *RQ* 21 (Spring 1982):247–49.

12

Developing and Implementing a Patron Behavior Policy

Linda A. Morrissett

A patron behavior policy is essential to effective library operation. Library policies are often written after the need occurs in reaction to a problem situation. However, a behavior policy is best put in place before the need arises. Remedial and legal problems can arise when there is no policy in place to deal with serious incidents.

A behavior policy offers several benefits. It protects both library patrons and staff from the abusive actions of others: excessive noise, threatening language or gestures, stalking, following or watching another person, and other disruptive behaviors that undermine the purpose of the library. It also lays out a course of action for library staff to follow when dealing with difficult patrons. A patron behavior policy protects the library patron's access to information and other facilities available in the library. If a patron is intimidated, annoyed, or harassed by another person's behavior, that patron may be unable or unwilling to use all or part of the library's facilities. Or, the patron may even defer any future library use because of an unpleasant experience, restricting his or her access to the library indefinitely. With a behavior policy in place, there is a uniform standard of behavior written to protect the rights of all patrons equally.

The library staff also benefits from a patron behavior policy. Clear guidelines defining inappropriate behavior and the procedures for handling it give employees a course of action to follow.

Library public services staff are usually fully engaged in their regular duties assisting patrons. They are often reluctant to approach a problem patron because they are uncertain how the confrontation will turn out. Employees may ignore the problem, causing further discomfort for other patrons. A written policy statement can and should be the basis for staff training to provide procedures and skills to handle disruptive situations. Giving clear guidelines to work with makes it easier for employees to handle problems quickly and effectively. An official, uniformly applied policy also helps protect staff from potential charges of harassment.

Having a written policy statement regarding forbidden behavior helps protect the library against liability and ensures the legal rights of staff and patrons. As long as the policy is written and enforced with a focus on particular behaviors and not on particular individuals or groups, such as the homeless or the mentally ill, then the First Amendment rights of patrons are not infringed upon. Court cases such as *Kreimer v. Morristown,* which challenged restricted access, often focus upon the fact that an individual or a particular class of individuals is being discriminated against. Having a *statement of purpose* for the library becomes an integral part of the policy.

Statement of Purpose

As a preamble to the patron behavior policy, it is important to include a library mission statement. The entire structure of the behavior policy should then hinge on this statement, from the definition of unacceptable behaviors to the basis for enforcement of the policy. Guidelines regarding behavior must comply with the mission of service as a whole. They must not be formed to bar a particular person or type of person from use of the library. However, if a person's actions do not conform to the stated purpose of the library, then he or she may be legitimately asked to leave. The person may even be barred from future admission to the library if such action is deemed necessary to prevent further unacceptable activities.

Writing the Policy

A patron behavior policy should be as specific as possible in delineating behaviors which are not permissible. Specific definitions and examples make it easier for the staff to monitor behavior and to take immediate action. For example, a statement that excessive noise is not permitted is too vague to enforce. Qualify that statement with a phrase about a level of noise which impedes other patrons from access to information or other programs. Give specific examples of what is disallowed. Consider citing the use of radios, typewriters, or computers.

The policy should also be written in as clear, concise language as possible while covering all of the major points to be made. Often quick referral to a point in the policy is necessary. If a staff member is unsure whether certain behavior fits the policy, it is necessary to find pertinent references quickly. Likewise, a patron who is asked to comply with the policy may demand (and has every right) to see the official policy statement.

A separate section should delineate the course of action to be taken when violations occur. Such statements would include the right of the library staff to remove the disruptive patron, call the police, and bar a serious offender from future use of the library.

Conducting a Needs Assessment

Conducting an informal *needs assessment* will lay the groundwork for creating a useful policy. Each library has its own unique combination of setting, physical layout, staffing, and clientele. While all libraries in general share a need to address disruptive, threatening, or violent behavior, the patron behavior policy may be tailored to the specific concerns of the individual library. The library's neighborhood and clientele should be considered. A public building in an urban location may tend to attract more homeless or emotionally or mentally disturbed people. A suburban location may have more problems with unattended children, especially in the hours after school.

In assessing the needs to be addressed by the policy, specific incidents and behaviors should be identified and adequately provided for. Many of these details will be evident from past or present experience. Look at past problems to determine what behaviors should be cited in the policy as inappropriate. Always keep the library's mission statement in mind as a guide.

It is useful to involve the library's staff in determining the kinds of details to be addressed in the policy. A general discussion sharing experiences and impressions about problem patrons may highlight concerns that have not been considered, as well as help from a general consensus on the "usual" problems. Staff involvement in creating the policy will also help them understand the problems better. The understanding and cooperation of the library staff is the key to a policy's success. If they are aware of the importance of maintaining appropriate behavior, they will cooperate with the training and enforcement necessary to implement the policy. Again, individual rights and library accessibility must be emphasized in the staff training program. With an understanding of these principles, the staff should be able to enforce the policy as a proactive measure, not a punitive one. Protecting the rights and safety of library customers should be seen as just one more aspect of customer service.

Defining Problem Behavior

It is important to clearly define each prohibited behavior. This way users will know what is acceptable, and staff will understand what actions they can take when a problem occurs. Definition of these behaviors may come directly from the results of the needs assessment. Some examples of inappropriate behavior that need clear definition and are commonly encountered in libraries follow.

Noise

Be specific about what sources and levels of noise are considered disruptive. Any restrictions on the use of devices such as radios and laptop computers should be indicated. Allow for normal conversation and activities at service desks, in conference rooms, or group study rooms.

Food and Beverages

Some libraries allow food and beverages, at least in designated areas, and this is worth serious consideration, especially in an academic library where students may spend long hours studying. If prohibition is maintained however, it is essential to enforce this rule strictly. Some libraries allow for the use of covered hard plastic beverage containers which are relatively spillproof. If refreshments are allowed, whether restricted to a lounge or vending area or permitted in the entire building, there should be enough cleaning supplies readily available to take care of the inevitable spills and crumbs. Barring refreshments from computer areas is essential.

Alcohol

Public intoxication, consumption of alcoholic beverages, and other drug use should be included in the policy, with reference to local ordinances or academic institution policies. Fraternity initiation periods and exam weeks are prime times for college students to smuggle alcoholic beverages into the academic library, and staff should watch for this.

Tobacco Use

Although the trend in our society is toward a smoke-free environment, special smoking areas may be designated. Again, the laws of the locality or institution may be cited. Also, remember to consider including other products such as chewing tobacco.

Other Disruptions

Minor annoyances such as animals brought into the library or children left unattended may create considerable disruption. If it is considered to be a potential problem for the library, such points may be covered in the policy. However, be sure the policy does allow for seeing-eye dogs or other pets which aid the disabled.

Theft and Mutilation

Theft and mutilation of library materials and equipment is a major problem that must be addressed in the behavior policy. Clipping coupons and recipes out of a newspaper is mutilation just as is cutting nudes out of art and photography books. Both are assaults on library materials and must be identified and treated as such.

In an academic library it is unfortunately too common an occurrence that a student is discovered tearing an article out of a magazine. Immediate, serious action is in order for this offense. At the very least, a formal reprimand should be given the student, along with a bill for replacement costs. If the action can be traced to an assignment, the instructor should be contacted and informed of the problem that the assignment has created. Some future violations may be avoided by enlisting the instructor's aid in teaching classes about proper use of library materials and access to copier equipment.

Security Systems

Library security systems warrant special procedures, since there may be frequent false alarms, unintentional removal of library materials, and even staff errors. There are some video rental stores and book wholesalers that use security strips that are not removed or desensitized at the point of sale. Patrons bringing these into the library will set off the security alarm when they leave. In any case, it is important to address patrons who set off the alarm in a courteous but firm manner while investigating the problem.

An obvious theft-in-progress should be dealt with more harshly, of course, while keeping in mind individual rights, safety, and library policy. Ideally, the alleged thief will be stopped, identified, and dealt with according to policy. However, sometimes security procedures will not stop the thief, and the best that can happen is that the library material will be left behind as the offender escapes. In such cases, it is best to remember that the primary purpose of the security system is to protect library property.

Loitering

Loitering is one of the most difficult problems to address because it is fairly easily covered by pretending to use library materials. However, persons not engaged in activities conforming to the definition of library business may be asked to leave the library. If the person refuses to leave, he may be charged with trespassing. Often loitering is linked to more overt problem behaviors such as sexual harassment.

Sexual Harassment

Sexual harassment may take many forms, from constantly staring at or following another person, to exposure to verbal or physical propositions. Often patrons are hesitant to report such behaviors because they are too timid, embarrassed, or shocked to do so. If they do not feel physically threatened, they may believe it would be overreacting to cause the perpetrator trouble.

Sexual harassment must be included in the behavior policy, and staff must be watchful for suspicious people who often feign use of library materials. If there are potential victims nearby—young women or men or children—special surveillance may be necessary. Here again, it is important to maintain the rights of all patrons. Obvious surveillance may be harassment in itself, so care must be taken not to infringe unreasonably upon an individual's right to use the library. However, anyone who enters the library who has already been officially barred must be told to leave immediately.

Disciplinary Action

Allowing undesirable behavior to persist without taking action increases the problem for both patrons and staff. Not only will unruly patrons think that they can do whatever they please and get away with it, they may quite likely escalate the undesired behavior. Consistent application of rules is the most effective way to maintain an appropriate atmosphere.

A policy statement should include a statement on corrective actions. In an academic library, these actions should be keyed to patron category. For example, students may be reported to the dean of student affairs; faculty to their appropriate dean or college vice president; staff to the personnel director or appropriate department head. In a public library, the actions should be keyed to the severity of offense. (For a discussion of legal ramifications of detention and surveillance in libraries, see Barbara Bintliff and Al Coco, "Legal Aspects of Library Security," cited in the bibliography for this chapter.)

It is important to consider when and how to restrict problem patrons from further use of the library. There may be an immediate decision not to allow a person on the premises because of serious misbehavior. If any restrictions are made, the person must be notified quickly in writing. In an academic library setting, a copy of the letter should also be sent to campus security and to the appropriate dean if the person has institutional affiliation. (When a student or faculty member is involved, the matter should be discussed first with the appropriate dean.)

A written policy should provide for police intervention. Illegal behaviors will require immediate police attention. Disruptive behavior, when the patron refuses to desist, can be defined as disorderly conduct and may merit police intervention. In an academic library, the campus police may be responsible for upholding the institution's rules and regulations. However, if there is no official library policy statement, they may choose to intervene in criminal situations only.

Policy Review

Once a preliminary version of the policy has been written and approved by the responsible committee or department head, review it with a legal representative and a police official, as well as a library board member and a representative community member. This review should ensure that the policy is entirely compatible with the law and with local policy. Police and legal officials may suggest changes in wording to strengthen the document. They will also help establish procedures for handling violations.

Academic librarians may meet with the dean of students, the university attorney, campus security officials, and one or more student government representatives. Students' questions and concerns can be addressed before the policy is adopted officially. A strong benefit of such a meeting is to establish rapport with those most directly involved. The dean of students will be more aware of behavior problems in the library and will be prepared to enforce library policy. Campus security officials will know that the library behavior policy reinforces proper, lawful conduct on campus. These officials can provide assurance that they will back up library staff in enforcement of the policy. As the rationale for the policy is discussed, student government representatives will have an opportunity to understand and support it as a positive document that is protective, rather than punitive, in nature.

Once a draft policy has been reviewed, it should be revised as agreed upon by the reviewing committee. If major revisions are made, briefly contact the reviewers to make sure the final wording is acceptable. Then the appropriate steps should be taken to officially adopt and implement the policy.

Implementation

All library staff who work in public service areas, as well as those in charge of non-public areas, must familiarize themselves with the policy as soon as it is formalized. Meetings that include security officials should be held to discuss potential problem situations and the methods used to handle them. If training sessions on dealing with problem situations are available, all public services personnel should attend.

There should be one key contact staff person to whom all specific incidents are reported. This person will also be responsible for notifying each service area of any problem patrons so that public service personnel will watch for them should they return to any other part of the library. The contact person can also recommend appropriate actions to take in dealing with a particular problem or incident. For example, should a man be suspected of following young women in the stacks, all stacks workers should have his physical description, know of the complaint, and be instructed to report any suspicious persons to their supervisor immediately.

One word of caution: even problem patrons have the right to fair treatment. They should be approached politely but firmly. Unless they are exhibiting dangerous or illegal behavior, they should be given the opportunity to leave the premises quietly. If they *are* exhibiting dangerous or illegal behavior, library staff should call the authorities immediately and not intervene further except to safeguard other people.

If the library has a security specialist on its staff, this person should be considered a liaison with the police department. A good working relationship means greater security. Even if the library depends on part-time guards for evening security, it is a good idea to let police know about the people you have designated to be in charge of the building. Having the guard(s) visit the security office for a briefing on normal procedures would also be good to strengthen enforcement training.

If there is no security staff in place, it may be beneficial to investigate hiring someone. Some public and academic libraries employ personnel to patrol the library, especially during evening hours. Personnel responsible for enforcement of the behavior policy provide a better atmosphere for library users and allow librarians and other service staff to devote their full attention to library services.

Recording Incidents

It can be helpful to keep a confidential file of information on problem incidents. (First, check with police and the institution's attorney for legal guidance on maintaining such records.) The purpose of a problem incident file is to track all serious problems that are reported, especially those that required police intervention. It can be quite useful in uncovering patterns of incidents to help identify the person causing the problem. For example, by keeping records of repeated thefts of backpacks or incidents of mutilation it may soon become apparent that one particular individual was seen in the area at the time of these incidents. Once the coincidence is established, that person can be observed more closely, and perhaps an offense may be witnessed.

The problem incident record will be helpful in relating details of an incident to the police, the library director, and any others concerned. It may also be used in decisions to bar repeat offenders from the library. (See sample form at end of chapter.)

Another good use of this file is to keep a confidential record of past offenders. For example, say a man was arrested and barred from campus two years ago for repeatedly following women into library restrooms. He returns to the library and is questioned about suspicious behavior. Once identified as a person previously barred from the campus, he can be told to leave immediately, with police escort if necessary. Again, this information should be used to keep track of previous incidents and assist campus police and officials. It must be a uniform procedure for all serious incidents, not just a method of tracking and intimidating certain undesirable individuals.

Preventive Measures

Problem prevention is much more desirable than confronting a problem with the potential for conflict. Handling disruptions is time-consuming and in itself disruptive to patrons and staff. During the needs assessment phase of preparing the problem behavior policy, some proactive solutions may arise.

For example, if the physical layout of the building presents easy opportunity for theft or mutilation of library materials or for harassment of patrons, it may be possible to avert problems by simply rearranging furniture, moving staff, or placing restrictions on the use of certain areas. It may be desirable to keep restrooms locked, with keys available at the service desk, or to place alarms in such secluded locations.

Good placement of service desks is important for general surveillance of public areas. Locking workrooms or other out-of-the-way places will prevent patrons from wandering into these areas for whatever reason. Having a staff member occasionally walk through problem areas in an informal patrol may help prevent undesirable incidents or at least bring them to light. An evening security staff is valuable for both public and academic libraries for prevention and control of problem behavior.

Newspapers, current periodicals, audiovisual materials, and reserve materials are prime targets for theft and mutilation. It is best to maintain these in high-visibility areas so there is less opportunity for destructive behavior. In academic libraries, such materials are often kept in a separate, staffed room reserved for their use. An identification card sign-out procedure provides a practical and psychological barrier to theft or mutilation of materials. Once personal contact is made with a patron, the area is no longer depersonalized and it becomes psychologically more difficult to violate social standards. Audiovisual materials should have extra security measures: either a special security detection system or a staff service procedure.

Food and beverage consumption may be an issue, especially when there are groups of students spending large blocks of time studying. It may be beneficial to consider setting aside a study or lounge area. If there are vending machines in the building or a fast-food restaurant adjacent to it, you will definitely have this problem. In this case, if you choose to forbid all food and beverages in the library, it will be most effectively enforced if there is staff near the entrance screening for forbidden food items.

Large, open reading areas are particularly conducive to noise problems, especially if the area is uncarpeted. Noisy groups of students are a frequent problem in both public and academic libraries. Breaking up study areas into smaller seating arrangements can limit interaction. Visual barriers, such as shelving, filing cabinets, or large plants, are effective means of preventing disruptions in large reading areas. Offering the use of meeting rooms and conference rooms for group study will be a viable alternative to disruption of a reading area. Bear in mind that some form of monitoring will need to be done.

In public libraries teenagers often congregate after school to do homework. Setting up a regular tutoring or homework assistance program in a meeting room with parent or service organization volunteers would provide community service and establish a monitoring system simultaneously.

If fraternities, athletic teams, clubs, or other groups cause problems each year, preventive measures can be quite successful. The library director may send a letter to the presidents and advisors of these groups each year, perhaps at the beginning of the academic term. The letter should refer to the policy and to past problems groups have caused and request that the issue be discussed at the first group meeting to establish appropriate behavior. This positive, proactive move is more effective than waiting to deal with problems later. And, once notified at the beginning of the term, these groups cannot claim ignorance if a violation occurs. Group leadership will be more cooperative because their assistance has already been requested. Also, working with the leaders of all these groups can be considered a team effort instead of an attack on a particular group.

Emergency Plan

The next step after creating a patron behavior policy is to prepare an emergency plan for handling crime and violence. Fortunately, there are workshops available to assist in awareness and training. Local law enforcement officers may be willing to present a brief workshop for library staff. They may also be willing to provide guidance in establishing an emergency plan.

Conclusion

In order to maintain access to libraries and library service, librarians must provide an environment conducive to research and study and one that is safe for all users. Library staff must maintain control of the environment in a proactive manner. The strongest basis for maintaining order is a policy that defines unacceptable behavior and provides for action to curtail it.

Appendix A

Western Kentucky University Library Public Services Policy: Acceptable Behavior in the University Libraries

It is the policy of Western Kentucky University Libraries (Helm-Cravens Library, Science Library, Educational Resources Center, Kentucky Library and Museum, and Glasgow Campus Library) to maintain an atmosphere conducive to reading, study, and research. Library and museum users must refrain from exceeding acceptable noise levels, eating, drinking, and use of tobacco except in officially designated locations, and/or from any other disruptive behavior which impinges on the rights and needs of others. Users violating these requirements will be subject to the following:

Guidelines

1. Any individual identified by University Libraries faculty or staff as exhibiting unacceptable behavior will be asked to desist such behavior or leave the library.
2. If this individual refuses to comply, the campus police will be called to handle the situation.
3. Information on each incident will be documented on a contact card and filed at the University Libraries. This confidential information may be used in any decision to restrict the individual's use of the libraries.
4. Any student who has violated this policy will be reported to the Dean of Student Life for appropriate action.
5. Any faculty member who has violated this policy will be reported to the Vice President for Academic Affairs.
6. Any other Western employee who has violated this policy will be reported to the Director of Personnel Services for appropriate action.

Examples of Unacceptable Behavior

1. Excessive noise.
   Examples: Loud talking, singing, playing a musical instrument or radio.

2. Consumption of food, beverages, or tobacco products in unauthorized areas.
3. Mutilation or theft of University Libraries' materials or property.
4. Disorderly, disruptive, or threatening behavior.
   Examples: approaching patrons or staff and engaging in unwanted and inappropriate interaction; threats to personal safety of patrons or staff; disorderly or destructive behavior, violent behavior.
5. Suspicious lurking.
   Examples: the person is not using library materials and seems to be out of place; the person seems to be watching other patrons or library employees or their belongings.
6. Sexual offenses.
   Examples: indecent exposure, inappropriate sexual advances or harassment (physical or verbal).

Appendix B

Contact Form

Please provide description of unacceptable behavior reported and description of any action taken (e.g., person was asked to leave and did so; police called, officer escorted person from the library, etc.).

Name ____

SSN ____

Date of Incident ________________ Time ________________

Description of Incident:

Reported by ______________________________________

Witnesses _______________________________________

Action Taken:

Submit contact form to Library Security Supervisor.

Bibliography

"ACRL Guidelines for the Preparation of Policies on Library Access: A Draft." *College & Research Libraries News* 53 (Dec. 1992): 709–18.

American Library Association. Office for Intellectual Freedom. *Intellectual Freedom Manual.* 5th ed. Chicago: American Library Assn., 1996.

Bintliff, Barbara and Al Coco. "Legal Aspects of Library Security." In *Security for Libraries: People, Buildings, Collections,* ed. Marvine Brand, 83–107. Chicago: American Library Assn., 1984.

Brand, Marvine, ed. *Security for Libraries: People, Buildings, Collections.* Chicago: American Library Assn., 1984.

Building Security and Personal Safety. SPEC Kit no. 150. Washington, D.C.: Association of Research Libraries, 1989.

Chaney, Michael and Alan F. MacDougall, eds. *Security and Crime Prevention in Libraries.* Aldershot, Eng., and Brookfield, Vt.: Ashgate, 1992.

"June 20, 1992 Proposed Guidelines for the Development of Policies regarding User Behavior and Library Usage." *New Jersey Libraries* 25 (Fall 1992): 22–24.

Lyon, Nina and Warren Graham. "Library Security: One Solution." *North Carolina Libraries* 49 (Spring 1991): 21–23.

St. Lifer, Evan. "How Safe Are Our Libraries?" *Library Journal* 119 (Aug. 1994): 35–39.

13

Literature on Library Patrons: An Annotated Guide

Beth McNeil

In 1989, Bruce Shuman's "Problem Patrons in Libraries—A Review Article," was published in *Library and Archival Security*. Since then, several articles have been published on the topic, and this chapter will serve as a review of the problem patron literature from Shuman's article to the present time. His prediction that library literature would continue to contain articles and books on the problem patron has proven correct. The problem of problem patrons has not gone away, although different types of problems are being reported.

One book, *It Comes with the Territory: Handling Problem Situations in Libraries*, by Anne M. Turner, has been published since the Shuman review article. This practical look at problem situations in libraries includes separate chapters on building security, writing manuals, and staff training. Appendices include more than forty pages of sample policies for meeting rooms, exhibit space, bulletin board policies, and more, from many libraries throughout the United States.

Other book-length sources of problem patron information include *Security and Emergency Procedures, 1991–92*, revised edition, by Northern Illinois University Libraries. Many libraries have emergency procedures manuals, and NIU's is just one example.

Published in 1991, *Access Services: A Handbook*, by Ann Catherine Paietta, includes a chapter titled "Patrons and Security," which provides descriptions of patron behaviors and offers advice on how to deal with less dangerous situations. The chapter also includes samples of security violation and accident report forms, other security issues, and a short annotated bibliography.

A. J. Anderson's feature column in *Library Journal*, "How Do You Manage?" has dealt with several problem patron issues in the last few years. Case studies on latchkey adults and on flashers have appeared in the column in the July 1994 and October 1994 issues of *Library Journal* and offer useful advice on ways to deal with these types of situations.

Two articles from the July/August 1987 issue of *Campus Law Enforcement Journal,* although older and not included in Shuman's review, provide useful information for library administrators. "A Secure Library Is a Blend of Technology and Cooperation," by Gregory L. Clementi, a Youngstown State University police sergeant, and "Survey Finds Library Security Problems Becoming More Complex," by Daniel P. Keller, director of public safety at the University of Louisville, discuss issues of problem patrons that relate to security at university libraries. Although not written from a library staff perspective, both articles provide useful information about problem patrons and ways for library staff to work with security officials.

Will Manley, in his columns in *Wilson Library Bulletin* and *American Libraries,* has offered advice on working with problem patrons. His "Facing the Public (Problem Patron)" appeared in *Wilson Library Bulletin* in 1988 and presented a tongue-in-cheek look at the problem.

In "The Problem Patron: How Much Problem, How Much Patron?" from the June 1990 *Wilson Library Bulletin,* Robert Chadbourne, a free-lance writer, writes about the Worcester Public Library and its clear-cut policy on dealing with difficult patrons. The policy and a list of instructions to staff is included in the article. An interesting sidebar to the article discusses the Haverhill (Massachusetts) Public Library's specially designed room to serve the poor and homeless.

Rhea Joyce Rubins' 1990 article "Anger in the Library: Defusing Angry Patrons at the Reference Desk (and Elsewhere)" from the *Reference Librarian* defines anger and responses to it and gives practical information for library staff on how to cope with angry patrons. Although the title indicates a focus on reference desk staff, Rubin's suggestions for individual staff members' responses and for institutional response are useful for all public service departments in the library. The reference list and bibliography include useful sources on dealing with emotions, people skills, overcoming frustration, stress, coping with difficult people, and anger.

Fay Zipkowitz, whose "Deinstitutionalized and Disabled Patrons: Opportunities and Solutions" appears in this book, has written previously on the deinstitutionalized. Her article, "'No One Wants to See Them': Meeting the Reference Needs of the Deinstitutionalized," appeared in the *Reference Librarian* in 1990 as part of a section on "Special Populations in the Library." She discusses ways that library staff can serve patrons with emotional, mental, and physical disabilities and describes ways that library buildings and equipment can be adapted to better serve these populations. In addition to her bibliography, a list of other sources is included.

In 1991, an article by Nathan Smith and Irene Addams "Using Active Listening to Deal with Problem Patrons," appeared in *Public Libraries*. Dealing with the skill of active listening, the authors provide five examples of problem patron situations and active and non-active listening responses to each situation. Chapter 11 in this book, "Active Listening: Alleviating Patron Problems through Communication," is also by Nathan Smith and updates this article on active listening.

In the August 1994 issue, *Library Journal*'s cover story addressed library safety, with "How Safe Are Our Libraries?" by Evan St. Lifer, and included information about security systems, book vandalism, the effects of crime on library budgets, and a safety/security resource list. Sidebars by Colleen McLaughlin and Wilda W. Williams discussed the March 1994 hostage situation at the Salt Lake City Public Library and possible ways to prevent workplace violence.

Sheryl Owens discusses proactive versus reactive responses to problem patrons in her 1994 article in *Library and Archival Security*, titled "Proactive Problem Patron Preparedness." She questions how to define a problem patron and whether or not libraries and library staff are part of the problem. Deviant sexual behavior, and why and how libraries encourage this type of behavior, is also discussed. Real life examples of problems and helpful, practical solutions for libraries are included.

As the literature of the past few years indicates, problem patron situations continue to appear and new problems have emerged, adding to the list of problem situations of which library staff must already be aware.

BIBLIOGRAPHY

Anderson, A. J. "Latchkey Adults." *Library Journal* 119 (July 1994): 58–59.

———. "The Flasher." *Library Journal* 119 (Oct. 1, 1994): 57–58.

Chadbourne, Robert. "The Problem Patron: How Much Problem, How Much Patron?" *Wilson Library Bulletin* 64 (June 1990): 59–60.

Clementi, Gregory L. "A Secure Library Is a Blend of Technology and Cooperation." *Campus Law Enforcement Journal* 17 (July/Aug. 1987): 6–11.

"Crime in Libraries." *American Libraries* 19 (Jan. 1988): 31.

Manley, Will. "Facing the Public (Problem Patron)." *Wilson Library Bulletin* 62 (June 1988): 96–97.

Northern Illinois University Libraries (DeKalb, Ill.). *Security and Emergency Procedures*. 1991–92 revised edition.

Owens, Sheryl. "Proactive Problem Patron Preparedness." *Library & Archival Security* 12, no. 2 (1994): 11–23.

Paietta, Ann Catherine. *Access Services: A Handbook.* Jefferson, N.C.: McFarland, 1991, 75–99.

Rubin, Rhea Joyce. "Anger in the Library: Defusing Angry Patrons at the Reference Desk (and Elsewhere)." *Reference Librarian,* no. 31 (1990): 39–51.

Shuman, Bruce A. "Problem Patrons in Libraries—A Review Article." *Library & Archival Security* 9, no. 2 (1989): 3–19.

Smith, Nathan and Irene Adams. "Using Active Listening to Deal with Problem Patrons." *Public Libraries* 30 (July/Aug. 1991): 236–39.

St. Lifer, Evan. "How Safe Are Our Libraries?" *Library Journal* 119 (Aug. 1994): 35–37.

Turner, Anne M. *It Comes with the Territory: Handling Problem Situations in Libraries.* Jefferson, N.C.: McFarland, 1993.

Zipkowitz, Fay. "'No One Wants to See Them': Meeting the Reference Needs of the Deinstitutionalized." *Reference Librarian,* no. 31 (1990): 53–67.

Contributors

Alison Armstrong began her professional career at the University of Nevada, Las Vegas, in 1990 as an instruction librarian and is currently co-leader of UNLV's reference and instructional services section. She has published and given presentations on library instruction and is a permanent member of the library's safety and security committee. She is an active member of the Library Instruction Round Table (LIRT) and the Women's Studies Section of the Association of College and Research Libraries (ACRL).

Emerita M. Cuesta is head of access services at Hofstra University, Long Island, N.Y. She has worked in public services for fifteen years and is actively involved in the Association for Library Collections and Technical Services (ALCTS), the New Members Round Table (NMRT), and the North American Serials Interest Group (NASIG).

Linda Marie Golian is head of the serials at Florida Atlantic University Libraries in Boca Raton. She received a BA in social science from the University of Miami and an MLIS from Florida State University, and is pursuing a doctorate in education, specializing in Adult Education. Golian conducts a semimonthly "Great Literature" book discussion group with a local older adult residential facility.

Mary M. Harrison is the education/psychology librarian at Morris Library, Southern Illinois University, Carbondale. Harrison has had school, public, and university library experience in Alabama, Nevada, and Illinois. She is active in the Library Administration and Management Association (LAMA) and in the Educational and Behavioral

Sciences Section (EBSS) of the Association of College and Research Libraries.

David Hollenbeck is the director of public safety/chief of police at the University of Nevada, Las Vegas. He previously worked at Ohio State University with the police department. Hollenbeck holds a BA in political science and a master's degree in public administration, both from Ohio State University.

Denise J. Johnson is the access services and government documents librarian at Bradley University's Cullom-Davis Library. She graduated from the University of Illinois Graduate School of Library and Information Science in 1981. She is a reviewer for *Library Journal*, has contributed articles to *Illinois Libraries* and *Computers in Libraries*, and has coauthored a chapter in a forthcoming book, *Managing Business Collections in Libraries*, to be published by Greenwood in 1996.

Patrick Jones is a branch manager for the Allen County Public Library in Fort Wayne, Ind. He previously worked as a young adult librarian in Cleveland, Ohio, and Springfield, Mass. He is the author of *Connecting Young Adults and Libraries: A How-to-Do-It Manual* (Neal-Schuman, 1991) and more than thirty articles regarding library services and materials for young adults. Jones is a board member of the Young Adult Library Services Association (YALSA).

Katherine Malmquist is the associate director of the law library at Cleveland State University. She received an MLS from Kent State University and a JD from the University of Toledo College of Law. She was formerly the circulation librarian at the University of Virginia College of Law and has been active with the American Association of Law Libraries.

Beth McNeil is currently reference services librarian at Bradley University's Cullom-Davis Library. She was previously serials and collection management librarian, also at Bradley. McNeil graduated from the University of Illinois Graduate School of Library and Information Science in 1989. She is a frequent presenter on reference use of the Internet and is a contributor to a forthcoming publication on Internet use in libraries.

Linda A. Morrissett is access services coordinator at Western Kentucky University Libraries in Bowling Green. She has worked in libraries since 1971 in both public and technical services. Morrissett has published several articles, edited numerous bibliographies, and been a frequent guest speaker on various aspects of access services.

Charles A. Salter is a senior health services research psychologist at Fort Detrick, Maryland, where he helps manage an international program of medical and biobehavioral research. He has published ten books, including *On the Frontlines* (Libraries Unlimited, 1988), and more than 200 articles, many on mental health issues. Salter gives seminars at various libraries and library associations on coping with mentally ill patrons.

Jeffrey L. Salter is assistant director of the Shreveport (La.) public library system, where he has worked since 1980. He is coauthor of *On the Frontlines* (Libraries Unlimited, 1988) about problem patrons and *Literacy and the Library* (1991). Active in Louisiana's library association, Salter has also published more than fifty articles, book reviews, and poems.

Bruce A. Shuman is editor of *Library & Archival Security* and an adjunct professor in the School of Library and Information Science, University of South Florida, Tampa. The author of six professional books and more than three dozen articles he has been a frequent speaker at ALA conferences and National Online meetings.

Nathan M. Smith is the life sciences museum librarian at Brigham Young University and assistant editor of *The Great Basin Naturalist*. He has written more than fifty publications on science and librarianship and presented numerous workshops on communication and interpersonal relations.

Linda Lou Wiler is the library development officer for Florida Atlantic University Libraries in Boca Raton. She received a BA in history and an MLS from the University of California at Los Angeles. Wiler created an innovative older adult program while working as head of the Blackstone branch of the Chicago Public Library.

Fay Zipkowitz is professor and interim director at the Graduate School of Library and Information Studies of the University of Rhode Island. She teaches a wide range of subjects but is especially interested in library administration and service to special populations. Before teaching, Zipkowitz worked for six years as the head of the Rhode Island Department of State Library Services.

Index

abusive language, 89–90
academic libraries, 75–83
  access policies, 98–99
  crime in, 87–93
access limitation of older patrons, 59–60
access policies, 95–99
access to information, 13, 16
active listening, 127–34. *See also* listening skills
addicts, 24, 26
adjustment disorders, 24
administration, 31–32. *See also* supervisors; support for staff
  failure to act, 120
  and third party harassment, 110–11
alcohol abusers, 27
alcohol use in library, 138
Americans with Disabilities Act (ADA), 68–69
angry or irate patrons, 78, 88, 129
anxiety disorders, 23–24, 25, 26
arrest of problem patron, 39
arson, 89, 91
assertiveness training, 119

barring from library
  disruptive patrons, 39
  young adults, 51
behaviors, inappropriate, 29. *See also* policies
body odors, 10–11, 13, 79, 97
  incontinent patrons, 58
Brinkmeier v. Freeport, 97–98
building configuration, 32, 143–44
  lighting, 91–92
  restrooms, 124
Bush administration, 3

chewing tobacco, 139
children, homeless, 6
classes of problem patrons, 9–10, 77–78
Clinton administration, 3
Commonwealth v. Downing, 98–99
communications skills training, 120
community resources, other, 69
computer vandalism, 93
computer workstations for older patrons, 60–61
confrontations with patrons, 33–37
  mentally ill, 27
  young adults, 47–48
constructive knowledge, 118
contact form, 148. *See also* critical incident report
conversion reactions, 24
copyright, 100–102
counseling for staff, 21
crime in academic libraries, 87–93
critical incident report, 73, 143, 148. *See also* documentation; problem incident record

criticism, 128–29
  by young adults, 52

death threats, 28
deinstitutionalization, 4, 21–22, 65–74
delusions, 18–19
descriptions of problem patrons, 40–41
determinations, 38–40
developmental tasks of young adults, 46–48
dignitary nuisances, 79
disabled patrons, 58–59, 65–74
disciplinary action, 140–41
disruptive behavior, 78, 88
  defined in policy, 139
  sexual activity, 122–24
  by young adults, 48
documentation, 38–39, 40–42, 114–15
  contact form, 148
  critical incident report, 73

emergency plans, 145
emotions underlying criticism, 129
employees working alone, 31–32
Equal Employment Opportunity Commission, 107
escalating situations, 35–36, 51
exposers, 90
expulsion from library, 38–39
external users of academic libraries, 77, 78–79

federal depository libraries, 99
flashers. *See* exposers
food and beverages, 138, 144
frustrated patrons, 130–33
functional mental illness, 22–23

hallucinations, 18
harassment. *See also* sexual harassment
  abusive language, 89–90
  Brinkmeier v. Freeport, 97–98
hearing aids as disruptive device, 58
hearing-impaired patrons, 57–58
homeless people, 3–17
  in academic libraries, 90
  and mentally ill, 27
homelessness, 3–6
hostile environment, 107, 108–9
housing, intolerable, 5

impulse control disorders, 24
inappropriate behavior, 29
incontinent patrons, 58
indifference, 5–6
interlibrary loan and copyright infringement, 101–2
investigation of sexual harassment complaints, 113–14
irate or angry patrons, 78, 88, 129

jurisdictional disputes, 5

Kreimer v. Morristown, 10, 30–31, 96–97

large-print materials, 62
Larry (homeless person), 7–8, 11, 14–15
legal issues, 95–103
legal reference, 102–3
library as safe haven, 69–70
library as social center, 45, 53
library cards for homeless people, 70
library staff. *See* staff
lighting for visually impaired patrons, 57
limits and boundaries for young adults, 47
listening skills, 72, 119, 127–34
loitering, 140

management concerns, 31–32. *See also* administration
manic-depressives, 19
marking in books, 62
medical reference, 102–3
mental illness, 13, 14, 22–23
mentally ill patrons, 4, 18–43
mentally retarded patrons, 25
mood swings, 19
mutilation of materials, 87–88

naming of patrons, 40–41
needs assessment, 137–38
neuroses. *See* anxiety disorders
nicknames for patrons, 40–41
noise, 50, 138
  and older patrons, 58
  preventative measures, 144
nuisance patrons, 10, 79, 89–90

obsessive-compulsive disorders, 23–24
older adults, 55–63, 79
organic mental illness, 22
outreach programs for older patrons, 59–60

panic buttons, 32, 91
paranoia, 25, 26–27, 90–91
personality disorders, 24, 26
phobias, 23
photocopiers, 100–102
physical activity, 47
physical harassment, 110
police, 142
  and sexual harassment charges, 117
  and threats, 90–91
  and young adults, 49
police, off-duty, 33
police intervention, 32, 141
policies, 10, 71, 146–47
  in academic libraries, 80–81
  and deinstitutionalized patrons, 70, 71
  developing and implementing, 29–31, 135–48
  and the homeless, 12
  legal need for, 98
  sexual harassment, 112–13
policies and procedures manual, 80–81
policy review, 141–42
poor people, 4–5
power tripping by librarians, 51–52
preparations for problem patrons, 29, 69
pressing charges, 117
preventive measures, 143–45
problem incident record, 143. *See also* critical incident report
problem ownership, 127–28
procedures, 80–81
  expulsion of patrons, 98
  sexual harassment complaints, 113–16
professors. *See* dignitary nuisances
prohibitions, 10
props in confrontations, 36–37
psychology, training in, 20
psychopaths, 24, 26
psychoses, 24–25
public library access policies, 95–98
publicity campaigns, 93

rare book theft, 93
reacting to security incidents, 34–36
Reagan administration, 3
record keeping. *See* documentation
reference services, 102–4
referrals
  in problem patron policies, 30
  to young adult services, 49
relationships with young adults, 48–49
restraining orders, 117
restrooms
  tearoom behavior, 123–24
retaliation, 115
risk assessment
  mentally ill patrons, 19, 25–27
  problem patrons, 9–10, 77–78
rude patrons, 130–31

schizophrenia, 24–26, 90–91
security, campus, 88–89
security guards, 32–33, 88, 92, 142–43
  in academic libraries, 90
  librarians as, 46
security problem areas, 32
security systems, 139–40
service desks, 143
sexual behavior in libraries, 122–24
sexual discrimination, 109
sexual harassment, 106–20, 140
signage for visually impaired patrons, 57
smoking, 138–39
social center, library as, 45
social contract, 66–67
socialization to library policies, 66–67, 71
sociopaths, 19
special collections, 93
staff. *See also* training of staff
  anxieties about mentally ill, 18–20
  gender differences, 51
  right to odorless workplace, 13
  support for, 20–21, 28, 73–74, 80–81
  and young adults, 48, 50
stalking, 88–89
staring, 96, 116
statement of purpose, 136

supervisors, 35, 118. *See also* administration
support for staff, 20–21, 28, 73–74, 80–81
surveillance cameras, 92, 124
systems mistakes, 130

tearoom behavior, 123–24
technology adjustments for older patrons, 60–61, 79
theft and mutilation, 87–88, 139, 144
third party harassment, 110–11
threats, 88–89, 90–91, 116–17
tobacco use, 138–39
training of staff, 31, 71–72, 81–82
  in academic libraries, 91
  and mentally ill patrons, 20, 71–72
  and older patrons, 59
  sexual harassment, 118–19
triage, 9–10. *See also* risk assessment

unemployment, 4–5
unpredictability, 19
unwelcome conduct, 107–8

verbal harassment, 109–10
violent crimes, 88
visual harassment, 109
visually impaired patrons, 56–57
volunteer placements from community agencies, 70–71

warnings, written and verbal, 38

young adults, 44–54, 144